A Model of Corporate Financial Communications

John Holland
University of Glasgow

Published by
The Institute of Chartered Accountants of Scotland
CA House, 21 Haymarket Yards, Edinburgh EH12 5BH

First Published 2006
The Institute of Chartered Accountants of Scotland

ISBN 1 904574 17 3

This book is published for the Research Committee of
The Institute of Chartered Accountants of Scotland.
The views expressed in this report are those of the author
and do not necessarily represent the views of
the Council of the Institute or the Research Committee.

Printed and bound in Great Britain
by T J International Ltd

Research Reports
Refereeing Process

The Research Committee applies a rigorous refereeing process to all stages of its research reports. The refereeing process operates by sending the initial research proposal to two independent referees (one academic and one practitioner). The academic referee will either be a member of the Panel listed below or an *ad hoc* referee. All proposals are also reviewed by the Director of Research who remains in close contact with the project. The two referees are consulted on the academic and technical standard of the draft research report. In particular, they are asked to comment on:

- the academic rigour of the document;
- the validity of the approach taken in the report;
- whether the presentation of the report identifies the key issues and brings these to the attention of the intended reader; and
- whether the document will add to the knowledge and understanding of the interested reader.

Panel of Academic Reviewers

Professor V Beattie	University of Glasgow
Professor J Broadbent	Royal Holloway, University of London
Professor J Haslam	University of Dundee
Professor J Holland	University of Glasgow
Professor W M McInnes	University of Stirling
Professor C Mallin	University of Birmingham
Professor H Mellett	Cardiff University
Professor M J Page	University of Portsmouth
Professor C Roberts	University of Aberdeen
Professor M J Sherer	University of Essex
Professor P Weetman	University of Strathclyde
Professor R M S Wilson	University of Loughborough

The Research Committee is grateful to all those who participate in the refereeing process.

Contents

FOREWORD

This report extends the previous work of the author entitled *Corporate Intangibles, Value Relevance, and Disclosure Content* (2004) which explored the 'intangibles' content of corporate financial communication and the significance of the value-creation story and intangibles in such disclosure. This report provides an insight into 'good practice' in corporate financial communications.

Managers face disclosure choices in their value-creation story between public and private disclosure and secrecy. These disclosure choices are subject to constraints arising from reporting standards and stock exchange rules and informal costs and benefits associated with each choice. Stable high quality disclosure is expected to lead to a reduction in the cost of equity capital.

The report identifies broad categories of value-relevant information for disclosure to analysts and fund managers. These include: the value of strategic options, both those recently exercised and those in the medium term to long term; the value of current operations; the value of top management in generating additional value; the value of confidence in top management, and the value of confidence in the quality of disclosure and its credibility.

The report then considers how these categories form part of the dynamic feedback process between companies and the market whereby such financial communications can change fund managers' and analysts' 'understanding and confidence' of a company and this, in turn, can impact upon the stockmarket. The market outcomes of disclosure, reinforced by subsequent one-to-one meetings with fund managers, feeds back into corporate disclosures. The report identifies this learning as the basis for a formal corporate financial communications policy.

Finally the report considers policy implications at the regulatory level and the implications for further research. The model of corporate financial communication developed in this report could be used as a basis for designing new disclosure guidance.

The Research Committee of The Institute of Chartered Accountants of Scotland, through the auspices of the Scottish Chartered Accountants Trust for Education, has been happy to sponsor this series of projects and is pleased that the results are available at a time when the subject matter is so topical especially in relation to the Operating and Financial Review and there is global competition within the capital markets.

The Committee recognises that the views expressed do not necessarily represent those of ICAS itself, but hopes that the project will contribute to the development of corporate financial communications.

David Spence
Convener, Research Committee
March 2006

ACKNOWLEDGEMENTS

The author would like to thank Professors Vivien Beattie and Christine Helliar, Directors of Research at ICAS for their assistance and comments. He would also like to thank the ICAS Research Committee, the reviewers, participants at the BAA, EAA who attended the presentations, and Isobel Webber who typeset the report.

The author would like to express gratitude to the Scottish Chartered Accountants Trust for Education for funding this series of research reports and to the case participants for their considerable contribution. The normal caveats on the author's responsibility for the contents applies.

Executive Summary

Background and Methods

This report seeks to understand how large UK companies manage their financial communications with analysts, fund managers and wider stock markets, and how their learning experience changes their behaviour in this regard.

The listed companies in this study operate in a world where they need to continuously communicate with fund managers and analysts in a competitive market for information both during the corporate reporting cycle, and as *ad hoc* events occur. They also face a world of change in their product markets and in their corporate value-creation processes. Holland (2004) examines how the content of corporate financial communications has been influenced by corporate perceptions of changes in their value-creation processes, as well as by major changes in financial markets. The same forces have come into play in influencing corporate financial communications behaviour. Demand-side and supply-side factors have been changing the nature of the information gap between companies and suppliers of risk capital, while these forces have also created a need on the part of companies to develop their financial communications capabilities.

Seven categories of value-relevant information (V1 to V7) were identified from the interviews with the companies:

- **V1**: information about the uncertain process of creating growth through strategic options (organic growth and takeover targets), over a long-term horizon.

- **V2:** information on how new sources of additional value are created by new strategic options exercisable in the short-term to medium-term.
- **V3:** information concerning new cash flows and earnings derived from the recent exercise of strategic options.
- **V4:** information about the value arising from current operations, current trading and immediate growth.
- **V5:** information regarding the way in which top management and the board, directly influence the level of expected cash flows and the risks in V1 to V4.
- **V6:** information on how top management and the board boost confidence in the company value-creation processes.
- **V7:** information about the quality of corporate disclosure and its role in creating confidence about the company value-creation process.

Elements V5 to V7 cover information about the 'hierarchical' (or board and top management) value-creation process, while V1 to V4 relate to information about 'horizontal' (or input, process, output) value creation, and 'network' (alliances *etc*) value-creation processes. These seven categories of information also provide a more structured approach to narrating the Corporate Story of value creation as outlined in Holland (2004).

The companies perceived that their disclosure activity altered attitudes amongst core fund managers and analysts and perceived that their financial communication about the value-creation information agenda changed fund managers' and analysts' 'understanding and confidence in the company', and these in turn impacted upon the stock market. There was a cumulative two-way learning process by the fund managers, analysts and company managers. Pressures from private meetings together with continuous and cumulative feedback from market prices influenced this process.

Corporate disclosure and the fund manager (and analyst) process of using objective and subjective evidence (company and external) to evaluate the company story, helped in building confidence in the companies' value-creation processes. This interaction between the companies and the fund managers and analysts spread information about a company's expected financial earnings and about value-creation stories from the core group of key fund managers and analysts to the market as a whole. However, this confidence was very vulnerable to company surprises and to changes in market sentiment. This 'fragility' was due in part to natural exposures to business risk, but also reflected poor corporate track records in every case. This fragility was also increased by high financial communications exposure if a company was always a focus of the public interest.

The companies perceived that fund managers and analysts played a critical role in intermediating company-specific information into stock prices, volatility, liquidity, bid-offer spreads and the cost of capital. The companies expended time and financial resources to probe and receive feedback on what information was in the market amongst fund managers and analysts and reflected in the stock price. Changes in the stock price were often the first observable feedback that problems or opportunities were being recognised by the market in the execution of corporate value-creation and/or with disclosure behaviour. As a result, the stock market reaction to specific corporate disclosure as well as general sector and stock market movements were closely monitored by the case companies on a continuous basis. Fund managers, analysts, and market traders further amplified this stock market feedback during their private interactions and dialogue with companies.

Stable high quality disclosure was expected to be reflected in the stock price and lead to a reduction in the cost of equity capital. This cost of capital 'information premium' was expected to remain stable relative to competitors with similar assets and market position, but which had a lower quality of disclosure and less interaction with the market. The market was thought to learn how to price company disclosure over time; the premium, therefore, included an expectation about future disclosure and information. Those companies with an 'information premium', that announced a negative surprise to the market were expected to experience a sudden drop in their stock price and an increase in the cost of capital. The companies, therefore, recognised that they had strong incentives to maintain high disclosure standards and to avoid surprises. Those companies without an 'information premium' were less exposed to such a shock because their more erratic disclosure behaviour was already built into their stock price. However, they faced a relatively higher cost of capital and this was perceived as representing a major competitive disadvantage.

A similar premium on the cost of equity capital was identified with the quality of the board and top management and was built into share prices as the market developed an expectation about the future quality of management. The companies, therefore, had to maintain high management and board standards and to avoid succession and resignation surprises.

The companies learned to respond to market change and developed *(i)* a high responsiveness to user demands and changing market conditions; *(ii)* a flexible disclosure policy in terms of public *vs.* private *vs.* secret information flows; and *(iii)* adaptable internal and external structures.

The companies decided on the nature of their financial communications policy as new information continuously arose within the company and its competitive environment that changed the corporate value-creation story and their benchmark measures. The previous relationship with the market played a key role in guiding new decisions about the timing of disclosure and through which channel to disclose information. This learning process and prior disclosure behaviour interacted with corporate perceptions of the business environment leading to changes in strategy and key intangibles. This changes the value-creation story, and so the iterative process continued.

Corporate opportunism was also observed in the companies disclosure policies. The learning and feedback process acted as an important market pressure to counteract corporate preferences for secrecy over private disclosure and private disclosure over public disclosure. Concern about managerial and company reputation and how these interacted with executive job tenure, job succession, personal marketability, and pay schemes, were important disclosure constraints.

Performance promises, targets and forecasts also acted as key constraints on companies to respond to growing shareholder wealth maximisation pressures. In particular, private and public shareholder wealth maximisation pressure set the boundaries on public and private disclosure and focused disclosure on shareholder wealth maximisation issues. Shareholder wealth pressures also stimulated the release of value-relevant information and the development of value-relevant information systems.

Chapters three to six develop ideas of good practice and show how managers can jointly agree their communication practices with their core fund managers and most influential analysts over time. Companies should recognise that they need to earn this 'agreement' with 'market forces' through a continuing quality dialogue with active fund managers and by being able to interpret immediate feedback from the stock market. Private disclosure, knowledge-intensive intangibles, benchmarking and many other elements in the financial communications model can be interpreted as a rational corporate attempt to satisfy such 'market forces' in a period when conventional financial reporting channels are facing problems of declining informativeness (Francis and Schipper, 1999; Lev and Zarowin, 1999).

Policy implications - at regulatory levels

The financial communication behaviour described in this report can be seen as a regulatory success, a regulatory failure and a regulatory opportunity. It is a regulatory success in the sense that the companies avoid the private release of 'price-sensitive information' which could immediately affect prices in material or significant ways. It is, however, also a regulatory failure in that it highlighted the deficiencies in the information content of conventional disclosure mechanisms, such as the financial report and its Operating and Financial Review (OFR) section, as well as those in public announcements made *via* the Stock Exchange. This provides a regulatory opportunity and the model of financial communications in this report could form the basis of Financial Services Authority (FSA)-designed guidance.

The insights from corporate financial communication practice might be of use in designing new disclosure guidance. Policy makers could require companies to disclose their 'business model' or value-creation story in the OFR using the three value-creation processes identified in this research and by Holland (2004). First, qualitative or narrative disclosure could focus on how top management and the board play a role in creating and protecting value in the value-creation process (hierarchical). Secondly, qualitative or narrative disclosure might usefully focus on how business operations (horizontal) and network alliances create value. The story or narrative concerning horizontal and network value-creation could be further structured around the status of strategic options. UK regulators have sought to improve the OFR during the 1998-2002 UK Company Law Review and in the Companies Act 1985 (Operating and Financial Review and Directors' Report etc.) Regulations 2005. However the requirement for quoted companies to produce a statutory OFR was repealed on 12 January 2006. However, this has been very much an *ad hoc* 'muddling through' approach to reform. The above proposal is more structured and would facilitate a common approach across many companies.

Company announcements of price-sensitive information to the stock exchange could also be rationalised using the insights of this research report. The UK Listing rules indicate many specific events that have to be announced to the market because they represent price-sensitive information. Holland and Stoner (1996) also identify other corporate price-sensitive information event categories from a study of UK companies including, *inter alia*, the launch of a new product, new investment, new research and development expenditure. Many of these price-sensitive information events can be placed within two major categories identified in this research. Firstly, they could be classified as actions and events associated with the hierarchical, or top management and board value-creation process. Alternatively, they could be categorised as actions and events associated with the horizontal and network value-creation process. Company announcements of price-sensitive information to the stock exchange concerning horizontal and network value creation could be further structured around the status of strategic options and the four categories of value-relevant information identified in chapter four. These would include many of the price-sensitive information categories identified by Holland and Stoner (1996) and would also relate to the release of information about substantial changes in the corporate story, or changes in the relative ranking or effectiveness of benchmarked value-creation intangibles, as well as changes in the risks faced by the company, and alterations to the status of strategic options.

Private interactions and disclosure can also be regulated in the same way. Fund managers and analysts could be asked to disclose information about their private question and answer sessions with companies, with the structure of disclosure based on the value-creation process. Regulators could ask companies to reveal which of their internal intangible quantitative benchmark indicators were of most interest to these fund manager and analyst users, and which external indicators were published by other information specialists but were not generally available in the public domain. Regulators might also ask companies how they assessed the extent to which their disclosures had a positive effect on the information market's understanding and confidence, and what measures or proxies they employed to understand this. Companies might also be required to disclose their policies on public *versus* private disclosure and their communications policy.

Many of the above ideas are consistent with the prior UK development of guidance on how to disclose effectively to the stock market (price-sensitive information guidance) and how to develop good financial communications practice with fund managers. For example the Myners Report (1995) advocated that private company and institutional meetings, and associated communications, should be improved in the interest of national competitiveness; it placed particular stress on improving corporate investor relations and improving business awareness on the part of fund managers. This could be extended to include analysts as well as fund managers, and should explore how corporate disclosure can be developed to improve perceptions and understanding by all information parties.

Disclosure guidance developed from this model may play a positive role in improving allocative efficiency in capital markets and in improving intermediation effectiveness. The model also provides a key context for other studies of disclosure and suggests many new testable hypotheses. These are discussed in chapter seven and appendix five to the report.

Finally, the model captures information flows of relevance to many corporate finance decisions. Such a model may potentially be combined with an investment-financing cash flow model (Brealey and Myers, 2003) to add a novel and dynamic information dimension to conventional corporate finance.

Chapter One

A Brief Survey of Relevant Research on Corporate Financial Communications and Disclosure

There has been much discussion within the literature as to what drives public corporate disclosure. For example, Schipper (1989) reviews the range of influences on the timing, information content, volume and quality of disclosed information, while Revsine (1991) outlines the incentives management have for the control of disclosed information. Lev (1992) discusses how companies can design and implement corporate disclosure strategy and notes that at the time 'managers rarely devote to information disclosure the careful attention and planning accorded to other corporate activities'. In practice, there are very few studies which directly interview or observe management in an attempt to explain the details of corporate disclosure behaviour and to develop more complex models of corporate disclosure. Gibbins *et al.* (1990) is a rare exception; the authors employ a grounded theory approach to understand the broad drivers and components of corporate public disclosure behaviour.

Holland and Stoner (1996) adopt a similar grounded theory approach to explaining corporate disclosure and management of price-sensitive information, while Holland (1997, 1998) develops an embryonic model of the broader corporate disclosure behaviour set in a UK context. As a result, a primary aim of the present study was to investigate further the detailed character of this broader corporate disclosure behaviour within the context of large UK companies operating in a major international financial centre, the City of London. The intention was to model this behaviour on the data derived from the case interviews and archival sources, and to expand on the prior grounded theory work.

There is a limited literature touching on how companies conduct their private voluntary disclosure to financial markets (Lee and Tweedie, 1981; Arnold and Moizer, 1984; Chugh and Meador, 1984; Treynor, 1993; Marston, 1993, 1996; Holland, 1994; Holland and Stoner, 1996; Barker, 1997; Holland and Doran, 1998; and Holland, 1998). For example, Arnold and Moizer (1984) highlight the value of direct company contacts for UK analysts and Chugh and Meador (1984) survey US analysts and also note the significance of direct corporate contacts. The latter study also emphasises the role of qualitative variables such as management quality and their role as intermediaries in the estimation of financial fundamentals. Marston (1996) shows how company respondents perceive the relative importance of private disclosure about different types of information on future prospects. Barker (1997) finds that formal and direct contacts with senior company management are the most important sources of information for fund managers, and that the report and accounts are the second major source of information. Meetings with company executives are particularly important to allow fund managers to understand the strategy of the company, and to assess management's capacity to achieve the strategy. Holland (1997, 1998) describe how 33 large UK companies communicated with their primary or core shareholders, the large UK financial institutions. The research focuses on the private voluntary information flows from the investee company to the investor institution (fund manager) and their eventual release into the public domain. This case work reveals that private company and fund manager meetings focus on a very different information agenda from that employed for the public channels. Marston and Empson (2004) in a survey of top 500 UK companies in 2002, revealed how active UK managers were in using informal channels to communicate information. These included various forms of meetings, such as analyst briefings on results and one-to-one meetings with fund manager investors. Site visits and roadshows provided another opportunity for companies to meet analysts and investors, but one-to-one meetings were ranked as the most important communication channel with analysts and investors.

The work of Marston (1993, 1996), Holland (1995), Barker (1997), Holland and Doran (1998), Holland and Stoner (1996), and Holland (1997, 1998) indicates that private corporate disclosure through one-to-one meetings and other informal channels are the dominant means by which companies seek to disclose qualitative information on intangibles. Holland (1998, 2001) reveals how fund managers emphasise the significance of intangible or qualitative factors in company valuation and in corporate governance. As a result, this new field research was extended to consider the role that qualitative information on intangible and tangible assets played in the broader form of corporate disclosure behaviour identified by Gibbins *et al.* (1990) and Holland (1997, 1998).

Outline of the report

This chapter has provided a brief summary of the literature relevant to this report. Chapter two discusses the case interview research questions and grounded theory research methods. The presentation of the model of financial communications and the use of literature are also discussed. Chapter three then outlines the major corporate financial communications choices in one period, comprising common public, private and secrecy choices; this chapter also covers priorities regarding these choices and opportunistic behaviour. Chapter four interprets the corporate value-creation story as a continuous process of creating and exercising options, and reveals how value-relevant information changes with the status of strategic options. Chapter five goes on to describe corporate perceptions of the impact of their disclosure behaviour on understanding and confidence amongst core fund managers and analysts, and how these outcomes are perceived to impact on the stock market, while chapter six explores how corporate learning about such market outcomes create 'a learnt context of preferences' which influence current and future financial communications. Chapters three to six as a whole provide extensive insights into 'good practice' in corporate financial communications. In chapter seven, the overall model of financial communications is summarised and concludes the report by outlining and discussing its key policy implications.

Chapter Two

Research Questions and Methods

Given the prior research and the nature of the research questions, a grounded theory approach was used for this project. It is difficult to investigate linked, interactive corporate disclosure behaviour by 'arms length' research methods such as analytic modelling or event studies. Given the nature of the research question, it is necessary to get as close to the phenomena as possible to collect data about the primary corporate disclosure elements and their links. As Gibbins *et al.* (1990) argue, the grounded theory method 'helps to ensure that the variables and relationships describe the experiences of those who make disclosure decisions'. In addition, this research builds on prior (Holland, 1998) interview work with large UK companies.

Locke (2001) notes that grounded theory research is concerned with the discovery of theory and knowledge through an iterative process between data and emerging constructs. This inductive, pattern-seeking methodology allows a researcher to both develop a theoretical account of the underlying phenomena and to also ground such an account in the case data employed. Ryan *et al.* (2002) argue that:

> (in) *case study research it is important to know that the researcher has adopted appropriate and reliable research methods and procedures. This is known as procedural reliability;* and *in case study research we replace the traditional criteria of internal validity with the notion of contextual validity which indicates the credibility of the case study evidence and the conclusions drawn from them.*

The latter criteria are critical for assessing the interpretative research reported in this report and the following paragraphs seek to provide the reader with assurance on these matters.

The research in this report was conducted in two parallel stages. Stage 1 of the research involved collecting archival data on corporate disclosure by each individual case company. The most recent financial statements, public announcements, and presentations to analysts were collected directly from the company prior to the interview. Web-based archival sources became important during the period 1997-2000, while public announcements were identified from a variety of sources, including the company and the London Stock Exchange, the quality press such as the *Financial Times* and other major newspapers were also available on databases. Stage two involved interviews with managers in 25 UK companies over the period August 2000 to November 2000. The UK companies represented 20 different sectors. Twenty-two companies fell within the FTSE 100 size group, two were in the FTSE 101 to FTSE 200 group, and one was in the FTSE 200 to 250 group (see Appendix 1). Twenty of these companies had already been extensively interviewed on broadly the same issues from 1993 to 1997 (see Holland, 1998) and formed a further set of archival data on the content of the private disclosure agenda.

Although this sample of companies provided a relatively high proportion of companies from the FTSE 100, the aim was not to provide 'statistical generalisation' as in more conventional hypothetical-deductive research (Ryan *et al*, 2002). The aim was to generate enough company cases to create the conditions for 'theoretical saturation' as recommended by Strauss and Corbin (1998) (*ie.* the point in category development at which no new properties, dimensions, or relationships emerge during analysis). Similar sample sizes had proved sufficient in previous related grounded theory work (Holland, 1998) to produce case data with continuous repetition of the same kinds of narratives about disclosure. Senior company managers were the only individuals interviewed; their time was scarce, however, and this restricted the interviews to 1½ to 2 hours length in each organisation. Financial communications to stock markets is dominated by a narrow, closed, small group of people at the top of large UK companies (Marston, 1996). These include the Chairman, Chief Executive, Finance Director, and the Executive Director or top manager whose special expertise relates to management of financial communications or 'investor relations'. Appendix one reveals that all interviewees were members of this insider group. The interview questions (see Appendix 2) were semi-structured and designed to allow the participants to interpret and describe the phenomena in their own way (Bryman, 1988; Buchanan, 1993); prior grounded research work helped to define these questions (Holland, 1998). The company managers were asked to discuss their disclosure behaviour with core fund managers and others in the market for information. The focus was on disclosure in this common information market context for the listed companies. Sector specific disclosure to expert regulators in, for example, banking or transport was not investigated. Taping was not employed due to the sensitivity of the topic. An analysis of each interview was prepared within 24 hours from detailed notes made during the interviews.

McKinnon (1988) and Stoner and Holland (2004) argue that explicit strategies should be developed to counter threats to validity and reliability whilst collecting data in field studies. In the present study, counter-checks were made between the interview data and archival sources where available. These included checks against corporate presentation slides or against archival sources for publicly observable events such as mergers or financing episodes (linked to disclosure) involving the companies. Multiple cases offered opportunities to collect data on how other companies viewed such disclosure-related events for other case companies. Parallel research work with fund managers over the same period (Holland 2001, 2002) provided opportunities to cross-check corporate views on disclosure content, behaviour and feedback processes.

During the processing stages, the interview responses of the various subjects were compared, continuously sampled, coded, and compared to each other, using the constant comparative method as recommended by Strauss and Corbin (1998). Sampling was conducted until theoretical saturation was reached, or when new information produced little or no change to the open, axial, and selective coding of grounded theory. These resulting codes were then checked to demonstrate that they were connected to original quotations in the source material and, therefore, provided traceability or grounding. Codes such as 'private disclosure', 'company story', 'understanding' and 'market feedback' were, therefore, grounded in the original data. The refined code networks were then used to suggest theoretical constructs and associated maps of causal elements that were constructed into a theory of corporate disclosure in the information market (Strauss and Corbin, 1998). An embryonic version of grounded theory (Holland, 1998) was used for theoretical sensitivity purposes when processing the data, and hence there was a cumulative approach over many periods to building the model of financial communications.

The grounded theory approached adopted here corresponds closely to the 'middle way' proposed by Laughlin (1995). The themes identified, concerning competing disclosure choices, the role of intangibles in corporate value creation, the use of the company value-creation story, of benchmarking, of continuous corporate interaction with stock and information markets, of market outcomes and of fragility together constituted a 'skeletal' theory which provided a conceptual bridge between the experience of the case companies and the many complex corporate disclosure behaviours likely to be observed in practice. The new financial communications model has, therefore, created a new means to interpret and understand how companies make disclosure decisions.

Presentation of the model of financial communications and the use of literature

Locke (2001) comments that:

The presentation of grounded theories similarly follows a format that involves the telling of theoretical elements and the showing of data fragments that instance them.

and also states that:

This format can be outlined as: summarise the theoretical frame – serially present each theoretical element well illustrated with data instances – summarise the theoretical frame.

In this chapter, the theoretical frame of the model of financial communications is presented as a 'paradigm model' as recommended by Strauss and Corbin (1998); this is a conceptual analytic device for organising data, for integrating structure with process and for summarising the model of financial communications. It links five broad modelling ideas of causal conditions: phenomenon; context; action strategy; intervening conditions; and consequences.

Locke (2001) points out that there is a problem of how to use the literature in the presentation of grounded theory. The presentation of literature in the early phases of the report 'mimics the hypothetico-deductive approach in which theory is '*a priori*'. She comments:

But what happens to how we write the literature when we begin with empirical data and hold existing knowledge in abeyance until our theoretical frameworks are well established?

She argues that:

... the answer seems to be that the literature which establishes the phenomena to be investigated still appears at the beginning of the

> *manuscript, even though it may be pre-empted by a sneak peak into the investigated scene.*

and

> *However, writing the literature in grounded theory differs from the traditional model in that literature is sometimes integrated into the presentation of the model in what is usually the 'findings' section of the manuscript ... Furthermore, the relationship between their grounded theoretical frame and a broader literature to which it makes a contribution is sometimes a problematic issue, because the research questions are not usually framed in terms of existing theory.*

The literature is employed in this report in three senses. In chapter one the literature is used to establish the phenomena and problem area to be investigated. Each major results chapter (Chapters 3-6) focuses on key model themes or elements. These elements are discussed in turn in the context of the relevant literature in appendix three. The overall model is summarised and in chapter seven the policy issues explored.

The paradigm model reveals how the grounded theory elements are connected and, thus, provides a 'map' to steer through the ensuing detailed results in chapters three to six; it should, however, be noted that the 'paradigm model' is an aggregate 'result' of these detailed findings. Case quotes are used throughout these chapters to illustrate these elements through interviewees' voices and narrative, and thus ground the model explicitly in the case data. The paradigm model is outlined in schematic form in Diagram 1.

Diagram 1 - Company disclosure process

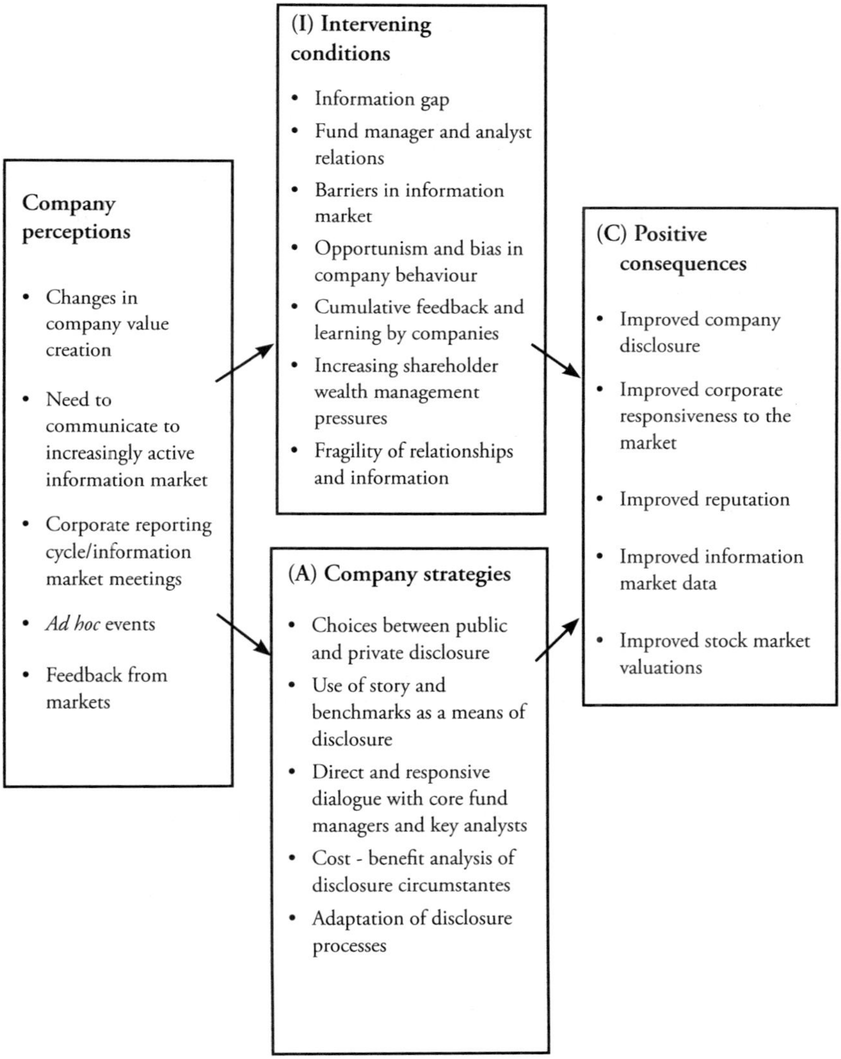

In narrative form Diagram 1 shows: corporate disclosure behaviour involves a dynamic interaction with the market for information and the stock market. The market for information is made up of companies, analysts, fund managers and other security market information users and producers. Companies' need to close the information gap with investors and other stakeholders by continuously communicating with fund managers and analysts in the market for information, as well as responding to the corporate reporting cycle, *ad hoc* events, and a variety of market feedback responses. Both supply-side and demand-side changes altered the information asymmetry between the companies and the market and the perceived costs and benefits of voluntary disclosure. Corporates had a choice between public and private disclosure and secrecy that consisted of a direct and responsive dialogue between a select group of top company managers with individual (major shareholder) fund managers and influential analysts. Cost-benefit calculations were at the heart of such choices. A story or narrative of corporate value creation, combined with benchmark information on the role of key intangibles, was central to this disclosure. The value-creation story was based on ideas of strategic flexibility (strategic options) creation and exploitation. Seven primary categories of value-relevant information were disclosed by the companies within the story narrative. Opportunism and bias were evident in this corporate disclosure. Growing shareholder-wealth maximising pressures and price feedback provided an important context for disclosure. This disclosure led to perceived changes in information asymmetry and in market outcomes. The feedback and dialogue created opportunities for (multi-period) cumulative corporate learning and for changes in corporate perceptions of the resulting market interpretations of this feedback. Each company discerned fund manager/analyst understanding and their confidence in both the company value-creation story and in corporate disclosures. This understanding and confidence were the outcome of corporate disclosures and of fund managers' and analysts' learning processes. The latter used concrete and subjective evidence to test the company story and to check promises which affected company valuations and acted as basis for the market understanding new information. Major barriers and problems were observed in this process. However, this understanding was very fragile with respect to company surprises and to changes in market sentiment due in part to natural business uncertainty and also to the complexity of strategic options and changes in earnings estimates and valuations. The interaction between core fund managers and key analysts and others played a role in driving market expectations and were aggregated into a market consensus. The companies perceived that fund managers and analysts intermediated company specific information into stock prices and affected the volatility, liquidity, and bid-offer spreads of the companies' shares. Changes both sudden and gradual were often the first observable feedback signal that problems or opportunities were being recognised by the market in the execution of the corporate value-creation story and in disclosure behaviour. As a result, the stock market reaction to corporate disclosure, as well as to general sector and stock market movements were continuously closely monitored by the companies. The case companies conducted extensive probing - and received feedback - in an attempt to understand what company information was understood by fund managers and analysts and/or incorporated into the stock price. The multi-period cumulative corporate learning and feedback process also changed corporate understanding of what the market wanted in terms of corporate disclosure. Cumulative learning over time generated a stable environment for corporate disclosure as well as the responsiveness and persistence that was built into this process. As new information arose within the company and the competitive environment about the corporate value-creation story and any benchmarks, the original disclosure content was modified and played a key role in guiding new decisions about the timing of disclosure, the choices of information channels, and in determining corporate disclosure policy. Visible use of company information was a signal about financial communication quality especially if they matched market norms for good practice; this learnt disclosure behaviour interacted with corporate perceptions of the real business and other key intangibles to change strategy and hence change the value-creation story, and so the iterative process continued. The consequence included an improvement in corporate communication (outcomes) and included, *inter alia*: improvements in corporate responsiveness and disclosure in fund manager/analyst understanding and confidence; in corporate reputation for disclosure in the market for information; and in the generation of a stock price information set that reflected the economic activities of the company.

This model will be explored further in the next few chapters.

Chapter Three

The Financial Communications Model - Corporate Choices between Public and Private Disclosure and Secrecy

This chapter outlines the corporate disclosure choices identified by the case companies. It presents a simple model of choice and the cost and benefits identified in these choices. The chapter also discusses how corporate context-setting factors, as well as company and market change circumstances can change corporate disclosure within this model.

In any one period or point in time, each case company faced a series of choices between public and private disclosure and secrecy, as well as decisions regarding the use of information reserves (concerning issues such as innovation or new product information), and how these choices and decisions reflected constraints. These choices are illustrated in Diagram 2.

The following case quote reveals that the priorities relating to these choices were established in the cases:

Insurance company case

> *Our disclosure priorities are: one, to meet the regulatory requirements in financial reports and in our announcements to the stock exchange. Two, to exceed these public disclosure levels by meeting standards for good practice and, where necessary, release extra information that is very important to the value of this business, subject to regulation. Three, we manage our private communications with fund managers and analysts and here again, there are external benchmarks in terms of good practice. There is also a benchmark in terms of what we said last year and*

the previous promises we have made and, therefore, we must develop information relative to these. So, in terms of private disclosure through these one-on-ones, we expect to exceed these benchmarks. … We give out as much as we can without breaking any confidentiality restrictions or breaking price sensitivity rules. Beyond these disclosure issues is number four, the issue of confidentiality and we will not cross this confidentiality and commercial disadvantage line.

Diagram 2 - Disclosure choices about the company value-creation story and their benchmarks

Public Disclosure

- Fully satisfy public mandatory disclosure in financial reports and in public announcements. Voluntary disclosure to meet 'good' practice.
- Place a fragmented story in the public domain and use narrative disclosures plus some metrics for key intangibles.
- Release price-sensitive information when major changes in the story occur or when strategic options are exercised.
- Continuously release news on the flexibility, competence creation, and observable company actions consistent with the story.

Semi Private

- Discuss public information in private, such as observed economic events, forecasts, results, corporate action.
- Fund managers observe these events and disclosures in the markets and *via* competitors, and probe in-depth in private.
- Companies 'signpost' fund managers and analysts to semi-public sources.

Private Disclosure

Focus on the wholeness of the story, signposting story elements in public disclosure, connecting narratives and the storyline.
Explain the detail of benchmark measures and changes.
Explain changes in the whole story
'Paint' a company picture to match fund managers and analyst's 'mosaics'.

Secrecy

Not reveal major changes to any benchmarks or to the central story especially if:

- There is competitive or commercial sensitivity;
- Management are at a disadvantage.
- The company is constrained by company culture, option status, and circumstances.

Therefore, keep a CONTINGENCY **RESERVE** of information for unexpected events and demands.

Public mandatory disclosure and voluntary disclosure

In the companies, public mandatory disclosure and public voluntary disclosure was managed first as they had no choice regarding mandatory requirements in the financial statements. The mandatory requirements included Accounting Standards Board and Financial Accounting Standards Board accounting standards. The UK Listing Authority and UK Stock Exchange disclosure requirements (1994) for price-sensitive information, and the Securities and Exchange Commission Fair Disclosure rules (August 2000) were the main external standards for public (announcements) disclosure outside of the reporting season. Price-sensitive information was released quickly into the public domain and information was also released to ensure that a false market in the companies' shares did not develop to satisfy all mandatory requirements.

Management then sought to voluntarily disclose enough information to satisfy the market. For example, since the late 1990s it has become a 'good practice' norm in the UK for companies to release trading updates about one month before the closed period, both for interim results and for preliminary results. Benchmarks have included requirements for textual disclosure from the UK's Operating and Financial Review (OFR) (Management's Discussion and Analysis - or MD&A - in the US). They also included regular public ranking of corporate disclosure quality by survey companies interviewing analysts and fund managers, and by members of the Investor Relations Society (2003) assessing companies. Corporate governance rating systems are also emerging which include explicit corporate disclosure ratings (Sherman 2002). Such voluntary public information releases are substantial during periods of good corporate performance and are reflected in the extensive use of images, text, graphs, and flow charts in a variety of media including the OFR, web pages, employee information and other public disclosure channels.

The companies, therefore, dealt with public disclosure first, responding to market and regulator-determined requirements for good practice in disclosure behaviour and content. The aim of voluntary public disclosure behaviour was to satisfy 'voluntary' good practice guidance and market benchmarks. This norm-based 'voluntary' disclosure often consisted of a significant volume of quality disclosures and was substantial during periods of good corporate performance or in periods of stability for a company. The aim of public voluntary disclosure was also to provide additional 'true' voluntary disclosure over and above such norms. Thus, public voluntary disclosure had both a 'norm' element and a 'true' element. The latter was determined by a complex, dynamic disclosure process involving a 'pecking order' between secrecy, private disclosure and public disclosure choices.

The 'true' voluntary disclosure information was released in an opportunistic way in public, but was still considered by the case companies to be fragmented in terms of telling the full value-creation story. In some cases a degree of fragmentation in the public domain was deliberate because the companies: *(i)* felt that its value-creation process was so different from that of others that it needed a full and detailed private analysis; *(ii)* wished to avoid a full or a faulty comparison with competitors; or *(iii)* they simply wished to maintain control over information.

Quasi private disclosure

The financial reporting cycle was a primary driver of an associated cycle of private one-to-one meetings with core fund managers (Holland, 1998). The case companies used the meetings to discuss public domain information including observed economic events and public forecasts, changes observed by the core fund managers in their real operational markets and with competitors and their recent financial results. The companies were also aware that fund managers and analysts exploited sector-specific disclosure systems where this information was made public *via* for example, bank or transport regulators. The meetings were used to 'signpost' these less visible public sources to a wider set of users. The private meetings were used to expand the fund managers' understanding of this public domain information and issues, as well as to explore the impact of external events on corporate performance.

Speciality chemicals company case

> *The oil price has just increased and, therefore, the question being asked of us again by the analysts and fund managers, is whether this raw material cost is increasing rapidly for us? We would argue that this is no longer true any more because we are no longer a bulk chemicals company. It is now only thirty per cent of our costs, and the costs of natural oils, palm oil, coconut oil, are coming down.*

Private disclosure: deliberate and voluntary to core fund managers and to influential analysts

The case companies also used private disclosure to exceed public disclosure levels. The companies were aware that core fund managers and analysts sought a unique information advantage and that there was no point to the private meeting unless this occurred. The underlying basis for such a release of additional information was the idea of 'relationships' or implicit contracting between the company managers and the fund managers, where the parties exchanged capital, information and influence (Holland, 1997) for their mutual benefit. For example, the fragmentation of 'true' voluntary disclosure allowed an extensive private debate to occur and created maximum degrees of freedom for private voluntary disclosure; it also created opportunities to 'paint the whole picture' in private and match the 'mosaic' needs of fund managers and analysts. The company advantage of knowing non-public or non-visible sources of information created opportunities to 'signpost' fund managers and analysts in their direction.

Consumer goods company case

> *Because the fund managers have committed to us we need to communicate to them in a balanced way so that they can see the value in the company. We encourage fund managers to 'look through the numbers'. This is a form of sign-posting in which the fund managers are helped to look through the various disparate numbers and it is also a bit of spin on our part in terms of looking on the bright side. So, for example, when we have this high rate of change in terms of disposals or brand harnessing and focusing or restructuring then these are rather messy situations and the information in the public domain is rather fragmented. This includes our financial statements and public discussion. We get the fund managers to look through the numbers to see the key indicators that show that the strategy is on track to achieve the aims. We get them to isolate the key numbers and focus on them. So, for example, we focus down on leading brand growth, and not on growth on all the brands. So, if there was growth on a non-leading brand that wouldn't be consistent with the story but if there is growth in, say, XXXX brand as an international brand then this is consistent with the story. We get focused down on earnings before exceptions. We focus down on the costs taken out to plan. We get them to focus down on where we have dealt with under-performing brand categories or businesses. As a result, getting them to look at the key numbers and relating them to the key elements in the story means that the fund manager sceptics can believe that this plan is possible. They can believe that we are making progress towards it. This is a central communication task for us.*

Fund managers and analysts also gained access to unique learning opportunities and sources of information when they could engage in an active private debate with managers and hear answers to their propriety questions. They could also directly observe management responses and performance in such private meetings.

Formal presentations were normally conducted in private one-to-one meetings just after the quarterly, half-yearly, or annual results announcements, focusing on concrete measures of financial performance and strategic achievement; targets for growth in margins and in Earnings Before Interest, Taxes, Depreciation, and Amortisation (EBITDA) for key businesses in the group could therefore be discussed. Growth in sales in central product areas, and increased usage of new distribution channels, were also popular topics. The meetings often focused on details of strategy, technology changes, growth opportunities, and restructuring and cost savings; these could be formally benchmarked against key UK, EU, US and global competitors, depending on the size and scale of international operations. Information could also be released on major areas of intangibles, especially at the more concrete, visible end and might focus on areas of brand management, customer relations and distribution channels, where the analysts would have access to their independent data. Chapter four illustrates how companies used their value-creation stories and benchmark measures to release both narrative (context) and specific information about intangibles such as the quality of brand management and customer relationships.

Retailer case

> *In the presentations, one of our main aims is to 'manage the conversation'. Nearly all City contact is done by two Executive Directors, as well as the Finance Director and the Investors Relations Director. We are all closely co-ordinated at our presentations to the financial institutions. We all use the same slides, the same words, the same presentation methods, and stick to the script that we have agreed. The script comes out of our strategy meetings and we get our investor relations staff to polish it up.*

The presentations used methods such as Powerpoint and made extensive use of time series graphs for measurable variables such as margins. Photographs and flowcharts of key parts of the operations, such as new supply chain technology, new distribution channels or new products, were interspersed between the figures and used to provide variety and visual insights into the company story. Written text was used but was subsumed under the slide summaries and subsequently expanded on the website and in the OFR in the corporate report.

Where the companies had full control over the voluntary disclosure agenda in the OFR text, graphs, flowcharts and images, they tended to 'look on the bright side' and present an optimistic view of the future. This control was at its highest in voluntary disclosure in private meetings with fund managers and analysts. Despite the mutual exchange benefits, the companies' preference was to control the presentations and their disclosure in the private one-to-one meetings with fund managers and analysts. Common text, graphs, flowcharts, and images were employed in the private meetings (large group presentations, and one-to-ones), and in the eventual published report, with the latter normally containing a subset of the material used in the private meetings. The companies recognised that they would prefer to disclose little or no information on downside risk areas such as the possibilities of major losses, or on a situation where there might be a major competitive threat to corporate valuation. Chapter six highlights the way in which market forces controlled this behaviour.

Secrecy

The case evidence indicated that many factors, such as confidentiality and loss of competitive advantage, culture, and complexity of the business, were major drivers of corporate secrecy and in altering disclosure behaviour.

Bank case

> *You can think of many factors driving corporate secrecy. One of them is willingness to communicate which is based upon the culture in the organisation and we are a poor example of this. Another factor driving secrecy policy would be the 'boffin' factor. The more knowledge-intensive and the more invisible the value-creation process, and the more difficult it is to communicate. This may well affect secrecy. Another factor would be the complexity of the organisation. So, a conglomerate spread across many businesses may have an issue here. Finally, ease of imitation of innovation may be a factor in affecting secrecy.*

A full set of quotes is presented because the factors driving secrecy were also major forces driving public and private disclosure choices. The quotes reveal much about these choices as well as about the tendency towards secrecy.

The following four cases illustrate the significance of secrecy issues in the case companies.

Property company case

> *Disclosure effectiveness has been improving but we can't improve this at the expense of other matters. We have no intention of breaking our confidentiality and commercial secrecy advantages and revealing to our competitors exactly where we make our optimum rental gains. We have no intention of revealing this to our customer base who may use this as a negotiating ploy. Remember, these are mainly corporate clients and they will certainly find this out and try and argue the case for reduced rentals.*

Insurance company case

There is a clear limit to disclosure. We do not disclose price-sensitive information in private, and we do not disclose commercial secrets in public or private. We only discuss in private what is already in the public domain. At times it is difficult to tell our story of value creation to the analysts. We may say that the insurance rates in some businesses are inadequate and we need to get them up. However, we do have some business where there are some very good business rates. To hold on to this business and to hold on to high rates we may have to reduce them a little and if the analysts find this out then they say, why are you talking about trying to increase rates when you have just dropped some rates? There seems to be a contradiction here. We have to be extremely careful here. We do not want to tell them where the good business is, precisely, and what the good business rates are. This may leak out and the competition will find out and go into the business. Alternatively, the customers will say, why have we been charged such high rates? So, we have to be very careful about the way we present the story.

Branded goods company case

We think carefully about the information needs required by people in the City to value the company. We try and ensure that they get it. We do not give them information useful to competitors. We do not tell them how much we have invested in new product categories and we do not tell them how much we will spend on advertising per product. We don't talk about profit categories or contribution margins per product. The point about this thing, if it is to go out in the public domain, competitors can use it to slice up this information and help them to attack us. If margins are down they can figure out how much we have spent on promotion and advertising and therefore guess where we are putting our marketing effort. We don't want them to know this. We do not talk about mergers and acquisitions before it is done or sales of brands or a particular production unit. Once the deal is done then we will talk about it. We do not talk about individuals. We do not refer to people as supermen, although we think our chief executive is pretty good. The business is the hero not individual people. We emphasise that our success is down to teams and not to individuals.

Retailer case

Secrecy is an issue here but we try to be as open as possible. We try to be as consistent as possible and, therefore, we think this is very important in terms of building up credibility. We say what we are going to talk about externally and agree on it and then we consistently talk about it and consistently report against what we have talked about historically. However, we do not reveal some critical areas such as store margins or turnover or profitability by areas such as health or beauty. We keep the information disclosure at a much higher, more aggregate level in terms of group and international level and not at store level. However, we do get some fairly nosy brokers' analysts who wish to go and see the store management. We find here that some of the store management do not know what to say to the brokers' analyst and, if you like, they are easily caught out by some of these specialist analysts. It is not really the store manager's job to talk to the City. Their job is really to run the stores. One of the problems we find is that if we let the analysts down to this level the nosy analysts will ask for the profit and loss of the store and try and get the store margin and try and get the payroll costs for the store. This is very competitively sensitive information and the competition would use this information against us. This is one reason why we set up a barrier here. The store management are not really capable of dealing with such sophisticated analysts and their questions.

Secrecy and corporate culture and conservatism on disclosure

Corporate culture concerning secrecy and conservatism, in disclosure was a factor in the cases.

Bank case

To a certain extent this is a cultural problem inside the Bank. Investor relations have been done by bankers implicitly as part of their other banking business. The question had been why do we need the investor relations profession in the bank? We don't really need this kind of activity to communicate our image out in the market! The bank was really unaware of the need to communicate this kind of thing. It had a willingness to tell the truth but its idea of the truth was a very limited supply of information. It did not spend a lot of time explaining the downside of the bank and this kind of information is critical for the fund managers to understand the quality of their investments. The bank did not really do this before and the senior management team now accepts that this was one of their weaknesses. At the bank until recently, management quality has been seen to be just a good banker not a good communicator with the City. This reflects the bank's cultural attitude to investor relations and to secrecy. Why do we need to do this, is a question throughout the bank. Why cannot we just get on with banking? There is a real education problem here. This problem has been made worse in recent years because of the increasing significance of intangible sources of value in banking. These are difficult to measure and this increases the problems of communicating these sources of value to fund managers, through financial reporting and increases the need to communicate via one-on-one meetings with the fund manager.

This bank radically altered its attitude to secrecy and disclosure after a major takeover battle when it realised that it had a very limited ability to communicate with financial markets; it believed that this had been the key factor in losing out on the bid to a bank whose more sophisticated financial communication skills were its only major advantage. Such a development in the case companies was unusual; most had learnt over time that undue secrecy had its penalties. In a few cases, a sudden change in attitude to secrecy involved a strongly-performing company with poor financial communication skills facing, for the first time in many years, a major crisis or a sudden decline in performance; this stimulated a move towards market norms for good disclosure practice.

Secrecy and the status of strategic options

The creation of strategic options that provided flexibility in the future was critical to the case companies. Information on how each company created strategic flexibility, and its subsequent exploitation, was central to the disclosure process. This creation and use of strategic flexibility can be interpreted as the creation and exercise of strategic options; chapter four explores this in detail.

Companies only released available information on a strategic option or flexibility when they exercised the choice built into the option; this was especially true if price-sensitive information guidance (from the FSA) or material information (from the SECs Fair Disclosure rules in the US) was involved. During the strategic option-creation process, the case companies kept the details a secret, occasionally privately signalling the broad nature of the strategic option involved, but avoiding the release of false information, especially false price-sensitive information.

The following two cases illustrate how secrecy varied with the status of the strategic options and its flexibility.

Retailer case

If we are researching Japan, China or Malaysia as potential targets and we are at the level of thinking about it, we will make a broad disclosure about this. This is not price-sensitive information this is just explaining our strategic thinking. If we decide to enter the market and to build stores then this is clearly price-sensitive information, and we must disclose this immediately and, therefore, provide full details. In contrast, if we are considering Germany there is a problem here. We can only go into Germany by takeover and, therefore, we are not going to reveal to our competitors and to anybody else what our plans are until they are concrete. This will only be revealed when we make the takeover announcement. You can see that it depends upon the significance of the decision for the stock price.

Oil company case

In terms of public voluntary disclosure then, yes, we do have a policy to manage disclosure of some matters where there are competitive and commercial reasons for not disclosing information. This might be problems we have or opportunities we have. For example, there may be a major opportunity in the Middle East at present, say, in Iran. We don't want to talk about it. Now this is a difficult line to tread in the sense that if we were to make a deal in the Middle East then it would be price sensitive and it would have a serious effect on the share price. However, the fact that we are talking in Iran or in the Middle East is not price-sensitive information until we sign the contract. It will not add value until we actually have a contract signed. As such we think it is quite reasonable for us to adopt a policy of secrecy when we are dealing with such matters before they become firm contracts. Once, of course, the contract is signed we have to make our announcement. So, yes, secrecy is important in the public voluntary disclosure arena and in the private voluntary disclosure arena.

The following case illustrates how secrecy and price-sensitive information varied with phases in mergers (as strategic options or flexibility).

Telecommunications and Internet company case

We do not reveal chunks of inside information such as our merger and acquisition plans. Investor relations are, broadly, appraised of these merger and acquisitions plans but we tell a different story to the City in the sense that we do not reveal what these plans are and we do not try to hint - positively or negatively - that this is going on. You can think of various trigger points during an acquisition or sale which would make us disclose price-sensitive information. Number one, the decision to dispose; number two when we are in discussion with other companies and possibly a leak occurs; number three when we tell the other non-executive directors, number four when the deal is agreed - which is really our preferred point of disclosure. Now leaks may occur anywhere between one, two and three and we might disclose if there is a major share movement. We can't deny if something is true. If a leak occurs then we have a standard release document and it is designed for the contingency if it occurs. If somebody asks us the question when the leak occurs then we say yes in the public discussion and we make a public release on this account when this outcome occurs. However, point four above is the right point to release the information and not point one. If we were to release price-sensitive information or what is deemed to be price-sensitive information at the point of disposal or at the point that we are thinking about disposal or purchasing another company, then ninety per cent of what we consider we do not do, and so it seems daft to release information about this.

If we published a list of who we might buy or sell then the price would go up. Unfortunately, it would drop later when we only implemented ten per cent of the list. Therefore, I think that points one, two and three are the wrong points to release price-sensitive information but point four is when a deal is agreed and actual value changes are occurring and, hence, the price will change.

The variation in secrecy with circumstances

The scale of secrecy and of the information that was held in reserve were revealed in various situations. The first was where a company had to go to their core fund managers to ask for help in, for example, a financing issue, where considerable amounts of additional information would be voluntarily released in private. This flow became a flood when a takeover battle broke out and the company faced a highly compressed period of 90 days during which it had to persuade its core fund manager that it had the best management team to manage the combined or separate sets of assets. Frequent private meetings were the common practice during this contested takeover activity.

Contested takeover case

During a hostile takeover bid, the battle for control is also a contest of ideas and these are the reasons for the dramatic increase in the flow of information between us and fund managers. The private debate between us and fund managers is competitive as the target company or other acquirers are doing the same thing. New information is created about the quality of the competing management teams, their ability to manage the corporate assets, their vision for value creation. We have to repeat our presentations to fund managers many times over during the takeover period and this can be a very boring and taxing experience for us. The quality of our financial communications skills is critical during this period to ensure that our takeover agenda is clearly communicated and we can respond to changing circumstances during the takeover period. When the fund managers have to make up their mind, they do so on the basis of the track records of the competing companies before the takeover period, and on what they have learnt during the takeover bid process.

When the case company management were asked whether this increased disclosure reflected either opportunism or secrecy, they denied it. However, the ebb and flow of voluntary private and public disclosures suggested otherwise.

Reserves and constraints

The case companies kept a lot of information in reserve, especially regarding the status of their strategic options and in areas of confidentiality and commercial sensitivity. These reserves were also held back for competitive advantage reasons and appeared to involve managerial motives to control information in the same manner as other corporate resources. In addition, the attempt to control the flow of information to markets *via* control over internal information was constantly 'disturbed' by unanticipated events and bad news/good news arising from external and internal changes. Thus, the internal information reserve was also used to ameliorate unexpected bad news arising from unanticipated events or to support unexpected but positive developments. Chapter five outlines how the perception of the 'fragility' in fund managers and analysts understanding and confidence led to the active use of these information reserves.

The disclosure of information within these secret, private exchanges, and in public disclosure choices was subject to the following constraints:

External

- The need to create public domain information to then be able to expand on it in private.
- ASB and/or FASB accounting standards.
- Stock exchange price-sensitive information, grey market and false market requirements.
- US SEC Fair disclosure and material information requirements.
- The nature of some types of information *eg.* easily copied patentable knowledge before or during a patent application and registration.

Internal

- Structural problems with own Investor Relations' (IR) systems.
- Commercial and competitive confidentiality issues.
- The extent to which a company had a strong secrecy culture relative to its competitors, the sector and the market.
- Managerial self interest and opportunism; managers managed information like any company resource, and sought to maximise company and/or management benefits.

The combination of these internal and external constraints were significant in the amount of secrecy prevalent in the case companies.

Costs and benefits in voluntary disclosure choices

The cases revealed a cost-benefit basis to voluntary disclosure choices in corporate financial communications. These involved the cost of information production, the propriety cost of disclosure (Healy and Palepu, 2001) and the range of perceived benefits. Examples of the benefits included: a reduced level of information asymmetry between a company and its core analysts and fund managers; a stable shareholder base; and a stable reputation for credible disclosure with analysts. Examples of the capital market benefits included: a high quality information set in the price (and, therefore, improved share rating and performance); price volatility reductions caused by a fall in the level of uncertainty; a narrower bid-offer spread; and higher liquidity. Corporate feedback benefits included a lower cost of capital. Table one summarises the wide range of costs and benefits identified across the company cases.

In the cases, some elements of these costs and benefits were identified as being useful in informal cost-benefit calculations for each major choice including public and private disclosure and secrecy decisions, as well as in determining the overall balance between these decisions. The company managers argued that they and their core fund managers and analysts came to some informal agreement over time as to: *(i)* what levels of disclosure were appropriate to close the public and private information gap; *(ii)* which costs should be incurred by whom; and *(iii)* what benefits were to be delivered in terms of corporate disclosure. Table one reveals a practical insight into the drivers of these decisions amongst the FTSE 100 companies in their financial communications. The case data did not facilitate an understanding of exactly how these costs and benefits were traded off in the case companies in the search for a satisfactory or an optimal disclosure decision. However, the observed 'pecking order' and its stability through changing circumstances, see next section, suggested that the case companies estimated that the net benefits of secrecy exceeded those of private disclosure, and that the benefits less costs of secrecy and private disclosure combined were thought to exceed those of 'true' voluntary disclosure. It also indicated that the firms gauged the net benefits of secrecy plus private and 'true' public disclosure to exceed those of high secrecy and conservatism in disclosure. The latter cost-benefit equation, therefore, prevented the case firms from adopting policies of high secrecy; regulation (of both price-sensitive information and the 'grey' market) prevented them from adopting a policy of only using private channels for voluntary disclosure.

Table 1: Perceived costs and benefits of financial communication by corporates
Information Market Benefits • Reduced information asymmetry with core fund managers and influential analysts; • Enhanced private exchange benefits with core investor fund managers; • Reciprocal information exchange with core fund managers; • Stable ownership base and capital supply from core fund managers; • Enhanced credibility with fund managers and analysts and improved investor relations; • Stable analyst following, lower analyst forecast error; and • High ranking in the market for disclosure, governance, ethical behaviour, and sustainability.
Capital Market Benefits • More liquid capital markets with smaller bid-ask spreads; • Lower volatility and less perceived 'over' or 'under' statement of price relative to 'intrinsic' price; • Smoother company valuation in the market and enhanced company debt and equity ratings; and • Lower issue discounts and less failures for seasoned and initial public issues.
Corporate Feedback Benefit • Lower average cost of capital through reduced information risk and better informed market valuation of a company; • 'Better' strategic investment decisions as understood by, and agreed with, investors; • Improved corporate ability to raise capital; and • Reduced vulnerability to takeover and reduced litigation threat.

Table 1: Perceived costs and benefits of financial communication by corporates
Propriety 'Costs' • Management desire to control information, keep information in reserve and avoid competitive disadvantage; • Non-disclosure of strategic options because of firms seeking control; and • 'Unnecessary' volatily due to premature voluntary disclosure.
Information Production 'Costs' • Gathering, processing and disseminating information *eg* costs of developing competitor comparative information, costs of investor relations functions; and • Top management time - trading off time on good city communications *versus* time spent on managing operations and performance.

Changing circumstances and changing disclosure levels

If 'normal' circumstances, such as expected or good financial performance, few corporate problems, or few external financial market needs are considered, then this can form a benchmark for 'normal' disclosure levels

However, the residual or 'true' voluntary disclosure element in public and in private varied considerably depending upon a wide set of company and market situations facing the companies. These situations could increase or decrease voluntary disclosure levels; if they occurred in tandem, then they could offset each other in some way, leading to difficulties in predicting changes in disclosure levels.

Company specific factors and prior experience set the **initial conditions** within which disclosure changed, was moderated or amplified. These included many of the company factors identified in this chapter such as:

- The degree of complexity of the corporate value-creation process, associated with a high or low number of strategic or growth options.
- The corporate culture of secrecy or conservatism in disclosure *versus* aggressive attitudes and managerial opportunism concerning disclosure.
- The current state of development, and sophistication, of corporate financial communication.
- Concern about managerial human capital and financial capital in the business.
- Other factors such as situations where the company was always a focus of the financial and other media and the public interest, for example, retail businesses, banks around results periods, and where the company was a national 'champion' or 'bellweather'.

A high complexity of operations, high conservatism, and a high concern about the managerial consequences of disclosure were company-side factors that reduced the tendency for a firm to disclose. Low complexity, low conservatism and the existence of few concerns about managerial consequences of disclosure all increased the tendency for a firm to disclose.

Company and market changes that **increased** disclosure levels included:

- The company feeling that its future prospects were not good, and deciding to get the bad news out of the way as soon as possible.
- Situations such as seeking additional market-based finance (debt or equity) or help during takeover battles. The enhanced public voluntary disclosure increased opportunities for further private disclosure.

- Any situation that increased the attention or focus of the market on the company; this included known points in the reporting calendar when the spotlight was turned on the company.
- More dramatic, but short, 'attention cycles' or 'news cycles' when there was a narrow market focus on a current 'running' story concerning the company. This could be based on major performance difficulties, other major company problems or, at extremes, a company crisis.
- Where the company was in a different situation to 'normal' circumstances, where the demand for information was higher and the company was forced to explain itself, leading to further disclosure; this was in turn likely to lead to more volatile prices during this short attention period or news cycle.
- Market perceptions about company-side factors such as high complexity, conservatism, and managerial concerns affected disclosure and could stimulate market attention.
- A major change in the disclosure behaviour of a competitor. For example, where an insurance company deliberately improved its disclosure on its reserves to create a competitive disadvantage for other insurance companies with weaker balance sheets, and to show how limited financial communications was within the sector.

Company and market changes that could **decrease** disclosure levels included:

- The company believing that its future prospects were good, where holding back good news would achieve the maximum timing benefit; this could be relative to shareholder aims, but could also be driven by managerial desires.
- The company not knowing its future prospects.

- Where disclosure would increase the threat to job security and tenure of top management or where it increased market attention on personal issues such as executive pay.
- A deterioration in company relations with core fund managers, influential analysts or their own house brokers. The relationship 'atmosphere' could switch from being an open, co-operative two-way dialogue with high-trust, to a 'frozen', 'chilled', antagonistic, and one-way, low-trust atmosphere, especially when company performance or other problems became acute (see chapter five).

Many of the latter situations could coincide with situations which encouraged disclosure, and it was difficult to interpret from the case data in which direction the eventual voluntary disclosure levels would move for a particular company. A profits warning for a complex high-growth company could have a major negative effect on stock prices; however, trying to increase disclosure on the value-creation story to offset this could be difficult for such an opaque firm.

Chapters five and six reveal further insights into corporate disclosure and counterbalances to corporate tendencies to reduce disclosure. It is important to note that the increased sophistication of information and stock markets since the early 1990s has generally forced large UK companies to provide much higher disclosure (Holland, 2004; Holland, 1998; Holland and Stoner, 1996), and that the companies faced continuing pressure to improve the quality of their disclosures.

Irrespective of the current disclosure situation the same model of disclosure choice was maintained. The internal information reserve was used as a buffer to ameliorate unexpected bad news arising from unanticipated events or to support unexpected, but positive, developments. The case data indicated that corporate reserves of information were huge and unlikely to be exhausted by such demands. The critical scarce resource was management time involved in financial communications and, as a result, secrecy was reduced by high disclosure but never completely eroded. Earnings figures alone (or with the OFR) were never the sole basis of corporate disclosure, whatever the corporate or market situation. They were instead backed up by the value-creation story and benchmark information which in turn were vital to explain the company situation especially when unexpected news or attention cycles occurred in the market for information.

Thus, it is clear that secrecy, the use of reserves, and public and private voluntary disclosure behaviour varied considerably with corporate and market circumstances. These choices were also driven by managerial opportunism and by managerial human capital and financial capital concerns. However, and despite this variation, all of the disclosure choices and the 'pecking order' remained at the heart of disclosure.

Summary

The model of financial communications presented in this chapter shows that the companies provided public disclosures first, and then satisfied private disclosure benchmarks (good practice public 'voluntary' disclosure), with the ultimate aim to control information for the company's (and management's) benefit. Thus, the release of information was driven by these secrecy, private exchange, and public disclosure aims. Secrecy dominated private voluntary disclosure because of commercial and competitive confidentiality and the status of strategic options. In addition, private voluntary disclosure dominated 'true' public voluntary disclosure, because of the private exchange or implicit contract benefits between companies and fund managers and analysts. This finding revealed a form of 'pecking order' or preference in corporate disclosure. Informal costs and benefits were associated with each choice of secret, private and public disclosure.

Opportunism was illustrated by the priorities for disclosure, as well as the way in which secrecy was altered in response to changing circumstances such as new financing or takeover bids. Opportunism was also indicated in part by the fragmentation of 'true' voluntary disclosure in the public domain and by the communication of a connected 'picture' in the private domain. The companies had a bias towards optimism in their disclosure behaviour and for avoiding discussions of downside risks.

These decisions were subject to many constraints arising from reporting standards and stock exchange rules. The decision choices were also moderated by the corporate setting such as corporate financial communication capabilities, the complexity of the corporate value-creation process, confidentiality or competitive issues, varying internal cultures of secrecy and conservatism, corporate tendencies to opportunism or bias and by managerial concerns about the human and financial capital in the business.

The corporate context also set the initial or prior conditions within which the disclosure changed. Many situations were identified that could increase or decrease disclosure levels. The situations discouraging disclosure coincided with situations encouraging disclosure and it was difficult to interpret from the case data the direction in which the eventual voluntary disclosure levels would move for a particular company. Despite these changes, the model of disclosure remained stable and provided a robust model to describe disclosure.

Chapters five and six reveal how these tendencies were 'corrected' by market forces in the form of active fund managers and analysts, and by an informationally efficient capital market. They also show how the information market and capital market pressurised the companies and generated major incentives for additional corporate disclosure.

This chapter indicates how companies can develop good practice in financial communications to further their shareholder wealth maximising aims. In particular, the data indicates that managers should establish their disclosure choices and the channels open to them and identify broad categories of costs and benefits associated with each choice. Firms should articulate their strategic story and clarify which information is subject to legitimate secrecy constraints and can use this to decide the level of disclosure in the public and private domain. Contingency planning suggests that companies should assess how this may be varied from normal circumstances to periods of financing need, or of takeover activity. They also need to assess how various changes will interact to stimulate more or less disclosure and they should explicitly address whether their 'relationship contracting' with analysts and fund managers is wholly in the shareholders' interest or is being driven solely by managerial interest. Over-optimistic biases in disclosure and opportunism should also be explicitly addressed relative to shareholder needs. Chapters five and six develop these ideas of good practice and show how company managers can jointly agree such decision practices with their core fund managers and most influential analysts. This 'agreement' is not optional for management in that it is normally backed up by strong market forces in the form of active fund managers and immediate feedback from the stock market.

Chapter Four

Corporate Value Creation, Strategic Flexibility and Information Content

This chapter begins by briefly exploring the 'intangibles' content of corporate financial communications. It also highlights the significance of the value-creation story and intangibles in such disclosure. These issues have been fully discussed in Holland (2004), where problems with stories and their dynamic and subjective nature have also been explored.

Chapter four extends Holland (2004) by interpreting the company value-creation process and story as a flexible and adaptive process of generating, waiting, exercising and implementing a continuous stream of strategic options. This 'strategic option' version of the corporate value-creation story and process provides a relatively simple and structured means to analyse value-creation processes across many companies. It can also be connected to formal valuation concepts by using an 'adjusted present value' approach to valuing elements of the strategic option creation and use process; this can be further developed by identifying cash flow categories for each element or phase in the value-creation process. Both of the latter additions to the analysis provide new means to understand the stock market valuation implications of new corporate knowledge-intensive processes.

This analysis creates a new and formal way of understanding the content of corporate disclosure. Such an analysis provides the means to link the information content of a more structured corporate value-creation story more closely to the stock market communication aims of companies and of the overall financial communications model. The data has been used to interpret the role of strategic options, adjusted present values and cash flows to the disclosure story.

The value-creation story and benchmarking

The case companies covered a wide range of sectors that have been heavily exposed to radical knowledge-intensive changes in corporate economic processes (Stopford, 1997). This exposure has had a major impact on the firms' disclosure agenda and exacerbated the information asymmetry between the case companies and suppliers of equity and debt capital. Companies, fund managers and analysts have sought solutions to these problems; the company cases revealed that the use of value-creation stories, of information about broad categories of knowledge-intensive intangibles, and the benchmarking of intangibles set within the story, were at the heart of these attempts to find solutions to asymmetry and disclosure problems.

Holland (2004) describes the nature of these hierarchical, horizontal and network value-creation processes. Diagram 3 illustrates these processes, which formed the basis of the value-creation story.

Diagram 3 - The corporate value-creation processes

1 **Hierarchical Value Creation**

Chairman, non-executives and committees who govern executive management

↓

Set of four interconnected and aligned value drivers: management quality, strategy coherence, effective executive pay schemes and quality of performance systems, which drives 2 and 3.

↓

2 **Horizontal Value Creation** → Cash flows, earnings and wider company disclosure agenda

input intangibles → **process intangibles** → **output intangibles**

3 **Network Value Creation and shared intangibles.**

In the case companies a specific group of intangible assets, such as top management quality or the coherence of strategy, were hierarchical, or top-down, drivers of the value-creation process. Executive pay was focused on creating managerial incentives to create value rather than a value driver *per se*. However, the alignment of strategy, management quality, pay and performance systems with each other and with shareholder wealth aims was a critical value driver in the hierarchical process. Each company articulated its 'horizontal' or operational value-creation processes that consisted of sourcing decisions and processes, transformation decisions and processes, and output decisions and processes. Within this process, the companies exploited middle management, employee human capital and other intangibles such as brands, quality of R&D systems, and customer and supplier relations.

The case companies also exploited network value-creation processes that involved sharing both tangible and intangible value drivers *via* customers, alliances, suppliers, and distributors, and these were mainly employed at the boundary of the firm. Holland (2004) highlights the significance of the story as a mechanism to disclose information about the above information agenda. The content of the story consisted of an oral or written narrative about how each company created value through these hierarchical, horizontal, and network value-creation processes. The story elements were also benchmarked in some way. Some intangibles, such as the effectiveness of R&D, could be inferred from absolute measures such as the absolute R&D spend and by observed innovations. Other key intangibles critical to a sector could be identified and their effectiveness ranked, implicitly or explicitly. This assessment was undertaken on the basis of a fund manager's or analyst's subjective judgements, relative to competitors or to the sector. Information was generated by privately observing and perceiving changes in relative benchmark indicators such as changes in the perceived ranking of management and their qualities relative to competitors, or the perceived quality of strategy relative to competitors.

Marston and Empson (2004), in a survey of investor relations for the top UK 500 companies in 2002, revealed additional insights into the disclosures in one-on-one meetings with analysts and fund managers. Short-term strategy, major new products and developments and long-term strategy were found to be the most important topics discussed relative to future prospects. The rankings were quite similar to those obtained in 1991 (Marston, 1993). Discussions about the creation of shareholder value were central. Most respondents strongly believed that the meetings were important for demonstrating the quality of the management team and it was also generally agreed that presentation skills were important and that management could receive valuable feedback at meetings.

Case concepts of flexibility, growth and strategic options

This disclosure was not static and its focus changed as both the structure and nature of company value-creation processes and changes impacted on the story. Crucially, much disclosure was forward looking in nature with a strong emphasis on how companies could adapt to change. In the bulk of cases, the firms explicitly used practical concepts of strategic flexibility and responsiveness to explain their value-creation process, to define categories of value-relevant information for disclosure purposes and to show how they were responding to change over time. These included innovation, or the creation of strategic flexibility, and of the use of flexibility, or of implementing innovation, in generating new products and processes. These were seen as the main sources of growth in current operations or the base case business.

The following case reveals how R&D was at the centre of the creation of strategic flexibility in the value-creation process:

High technology company case

We can be seen as a business involved in the creation and use of strategic options. We are in the business of creating a series of strategic options, one leading on to the other. We can start with our R&D activity focusing on engine or power unit technology. This focuses on the infrastructure of the engines and the integration of the whole engine system. We try to create our own monopoly advantage in the form of knowledge concerning the core parts of the engine design. This R&D effort leads to the capability to build a range of engines or power units going from very low levels of fifteen thousand BTU up to over one hundred thousand BTU. There are generic technologies and knowledge at work across these engines that are unique to us. So the new engine technology creates choices and flexibility in engine design and this is the key to having a common technology, a common design across the engines. These engines are usable across a wide range of industries and markets and this includes civil aviation, defence aviation, marine, including civil and defence uses, and energy businesses. The point is the same, engines have multiple uses and sales are made in each of these different market sectors. Sales are based upon the quality of the engines. We have unique energy use in the engines in terms of low waste of energy, low pollution and can offer a range of scaled-up, step-up, energy generation levels for each of these uses. It is this special edge in the quality of the product that creates the sales. The high quality of the engine technology creates choices for our marketing people when selling the engines. It gives them the ability to tailor the engines to the needs of airlines, defence contractors or of oil companies. This is a very, very important capability and it means that they can clinch the deal so there is flexibility built into the engines in terms of adapting them for the customer and clinching the sales.

R&D effectiveness or brand management skills in each company existed in individuals and teams, and were based on long-term learning in each company. For example, the existing corporate product innovation and launch skills were based on accumulated tacit and explicit knowledge of prior risky situations. These skills and knowledge were exploited within explicit procedures designed to manage these situations.

Such strategic options or flexibilities were typically based on combinations of key intangible value drivers in the case companies. Typically, the creation of strategic flexibility was driven by the combination of top management quality, and other strategic factors such as R&D effectiveness or brand management quality. Top management were monitored through shareholder wealth-oriented performance measurement systems and managers were given strong pay and bonus incentives to pursue such behaviour. In other examples, existing capabilities were combined with other new or existing capabilities such as brand management skills and brand power in novel ways, to create new strategic choices in product markets. In the following cases the traditional sources of innovation were combined with new intangibles to create new strategic options.

Consumers goods company case

> *Our strategy and its direct matching to our brands, brand marketing and brand management are key strengths of this company. They all create the strategic choices that we can exercise in years to come in a way that we think will create the growth in this business. For example, under our master brand we expect to create many new products and we expect to use the marketing skills we have to exploit the new brands we have bought through acquisitions.*

Insurance company case

> *The traditional skills or intangibles in this business are to do with underwriting, claims management, risk management and asset management. We are now adding new kinds of skills and intangibles in terms of brand management and marketing. Our underwriters assess new kinds of risks, price them and this experimentation has created new kinds of product. The only problem here is that sometimes the new product is poorly understood and we end up with underwriting very bad risks. We have now copied other companies outside insurance and use a product development and innovation group. They develop new ideas for insurance and risk and then assess the risk. This is a reverse of the way insurance underwriting innovated in the past. There are two different directions for innovation, one from the traditional skills*

and one from the new kind of skills. This is a good example of the interaction between the new and the more traditional intangibles in this business. We are also trying to manage risks better by using our old skills and intangibles more effectively. Our customers pay premiums to insure against risk but if we work with them to reduce these risks we will all be better off. For example, our US corporate insurer has a policy of a zero accident culture at work. It works with businesses to reduce the number of accidents and this can be combined with claims initiatives to produce above average performance even from risks that seemed unattractive. The programme brings corporate customers the kind of benefits not normally associated with insurance, such as improved work force morale and reduced time lost through injuries.

We are also trying to improve the management of our claims management. … We can use this improved claims experience as a selling proposition to the customer. We think if a customer is satisfied with their claims experience with us then they are more likely to come back for repeat business and to try out some of our other products. We are competing with a high degree of economic rationality in the market where people can search the website for the least cost insurance service. Therefore, if we can build up this intangible of customer satisfaction by a good claims management system which is both low cost and effective, then we think that we can provide some kind of stickiness with our customers and they won't be as economically rational by searching through the web.

Real-option flexibility was also enhanced by developing financial flexibility, as shown in the high technology company case.

High technology company case

We also develop new customer-end options through new financial and maintenance packages, and by using new technology to deliver services. This deepens customer relationships and allows us to sell higher margin products. For example, we have developed a new type of after-sales service contract. Once the engine goes into operation with an airline the airline has a choice. It can own the engine itself and maintain itself and buy the spares parts from us. This is profitable for us just selling the spare parts. Alternatively, the airline can buy the maintenance and the spare parts from us when things are required to be repaired. Alternatively, it can go further and buy a full package in which we ensure the engines are always operating and that the airline company doesn't have to think at all about spotting maintenance requirements and buying spares. We do all of this. This gives a very predictable cost for the customer. It also gives a predictable and high margin income for us.

The case companies argued that the market valued the unique competencies and flexibility that they built into their value-creation processes. The unique competencies embodied in individuals and teams were a primary source of the level of cash flows and earnings expected to arise over time from the normal operations of the business. Strategic flexibility was the primary source of growth in the level of earnings and cash flows and in finding new ways of managing risk. The case companies perceived that the market was continuously testing whether they had this flexibility and exercised it in an effective way over time. Flexibility and track record were assessed using objective measures such as: *(i)* R&D expenditure associated with new products successfully brought to the market; *(ii)* brand management expenditure and successful expansion of existing brands, established or new, across product areas new to the company; and *(iii)* brand expenditure and the establishment of new brands in company, established or new, product areas. They were also assessed using subjective relative rankings of key competitive advantage intangibles, such as, management quality. The bulk of the case managers had an explicit understanding of their company's unique flexibility and competence - and their contribution to value - and communicated these to fund managers and analysts *via* the story and benchmarks.

Option creation

Strategic flexibility corresponded to a growing literature which suggests that option theory can be applied to real strategic options. Writers such as Myers and Majd (1983) analysed the value of an option for the abandonment of capital projects. Levent (in Nichols, 1994) showed how Merck used option theory to value R&D in a pharmaceutical company. Four common real options identified as being attached to many capital investment projects are: *(i)* the option to make follow-on investments; *(ii)* the option to abandon a project, *(iii)* the option to wait before investing; and *(iv)* the option to change either the output or the production methods (Brealey and Myers, 2003).

Such individual option types were evident in the case companies. However, the case companies went beyond static concepts of individual options and projects; they identified the corporate value-creation process as a continuous process of creating strategic flexibility, always waiting for opportune moments to exploit this advantage and of it actually being exploited.

In addition, a small group of five case companies, one each in the banking, oil, pharmaceuticals, utilities, and speciality chemicals sectors, extended the concept of strategic flexibility by explicitly using the language of strategic options to understand and manage the growth and flexibility dimensions of the business. This development, in turn, altered the language of disclosure as the firms used an options perspective to explain their value-creation processes to fund managers, analysts and others, as well as the way in which these generated new risky cash flows and earnings. The five 'option' case companies viewed the company value creation as being made up of additional dimensions such as: *(i)* the creation of strategic flexibilities and unique competencies; *(ii)* the ability to wait to use this flexibility and competence (*ie*. exploiting 'first mover' status); and *(iii)* the initial use of this flexibility and special competence. These 'option' case companies exercised these strategic options, flexibilities and competencies, at key strategic decision points during their value-creation processes, such as when they expected an upturn in the market or a period of weakness in a competitor. The initial exercise, or use of the strategic option, was followed by a full exploitation phase or possibly abandonment after a trial period. The newly created strategic options were identified as a potential source of growth and hence the growth component of stock value. Once exercised and fully utilised, the options became projects in the existing business and the source of the base case value.

The case companies using the language of strategic flexibility and the formal language of strategic options, had continuous processes of option creation and exercise. This idea is illustrated in diagram four. The case companies invested in a continuous stream of investments that created a continuous stream of valuable strategic options or flexibilities, that were followed by a period where the companies waited for opportunities to exploit them. At some point, companies exercised their strategic options and appropriated returns from these knowledge-intensive assets. The regular exercise of these options was seen as a means to create knowledge-intensive barriers to entry that were costly for competitors to replicate. External events and internal discoveries or new concepts continuously altered the perceptions of whether newly created options were likely to be profitable to exercise 'in the money' or loss makers 'out of the money'. Further down the value-creation chain, the companies continuously paid exercise prices in the form of further investment in "in the money" options. This matched a continuously changing competitive environment, and the companies continuously exercised options or rejected options through time to reflect new events. The final exercised options created the unique, difficult to imitate, goods and services, providing knowledge-intensive barriers to entry, and a strong-lock hold over future market share and pricing. This, in turn, generated a steady cash flow stream which was then continuously fed back into the discovery or concept-creation process. Cash flow changes occurred in each phase of Diagram 4 as companies used and generated cash in different ways. A continuous analysis of the final market for goods and services also provided the feedback to continuously stimulate the creation of new options.

Diagram 4 - The company value-creation as a continuous option creation, exercise, use and abandonment process

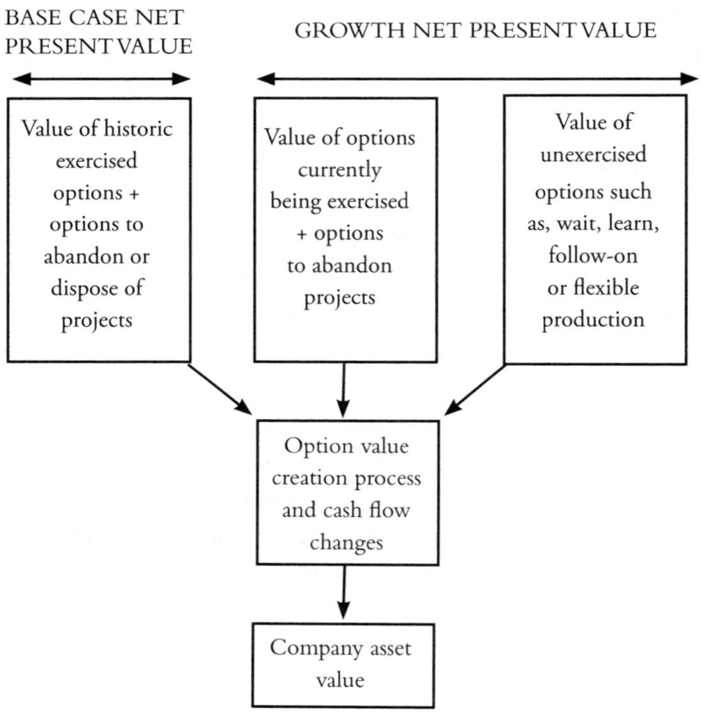

Practical case examples of the continuous option value-creation process

The continuous option creation process can be illustrated through the following two case examples:

Bank case

> *The important information I need to get over to fund managers are the competence of the management team, the coherence and consistency of our strategy, and how we are going to create growth by generating strategic options and then implementing them. ... The management team here is experienced in thinking out these new strategic options and this capability is clearly in our market price. We also have a good track record in implementing these strategic options. This also contributes to our share price. These ideas of strategic option creation did not exist in this sector ten years ago and this problem was linked to the poor quality of top management who were just occupying administrative positions rather than creating value. Strategic option creation has now become an important activity at the top management end of this sector and is also developing lower down in the functional units. However, we need better ways of monitoring the development of such options in the operating units and bringing them up to top management and board level for wider exploitation. This monitoring and exploitation of bottom-up option creation is central to a pharmaceuticals company, but is only developing in our sector.*

Speciality chemicals company case

> *We have a value-creation process running along from research and development through the application chemists or technologists, through the creative staff and then onwards to the customer,*

service and support staff and marketing and brand management staff and through to customer relations. This all leads to the sales, growth of sales, and market share, which all leads to the cash flows and financial performance. This is a complex value chain in a knowledge intensive industry. Each point along the chain has a high degree of scientific, commercial and technical knowledge in the creation of new products and creating value and making profits. We can consider each point in our value chain in detail. Our research and development has three fundamental science bases with coatings science in the paints group, polymer chemistry in our adhesives and sealants group, and sensory science in our perfume, fragrance and food group. Polymer chemistry is critical to these speciality chemical businesses, all three of them. Across these areas we spend between four and six per cent of sales on research and development and a high proportion of our products are patented. The science bases and the scale of research and development are critical to our ability to innovate. The three fundamental science bases form the technological platform for the engineers and applied chemists here. There is a group-wide board responsible for development of the group technology strategy and its delivery through the research and development capabilities which are distributed amongst the individual businesses. However, each major business is very much in control of its own research and development and its own technology application areas and for driving innovation to meet the needs of its customers and markets. Each group is very much focused down on the end market user, be they a corporate or a retail customer, and their needs and preferences. Therefore, information from the customer end, works its way back along the chain, back through the product innovation, through to the technology, through to the basic science to find out what kind of new knowledge is required to satisfy these market needs.

Pharmaceutical company case

The following case reveals how a company explained the continuous process by which options were created and exercised:

> *At the basic end in terms of R&D the analysts will be interested in the productivity of R&D. What is the size of the R&D spend and what is the chances of producing a certain number of new molecules and drugs per one hundred thousand pounds of expenditure? So, the question here is what is the productivity of the basic science? They will then move along the chain and look at the productivity of the other areas. For example, at the discovery point they will want to know how good are we at picking out candidate drugs for further clinical studies but these are the simple level clinical studies. Then when we go through to clinical development and regulatory approval stage they will want to know how we manage this. How good are we at managing large clinical studies and how effective are we at getting drugs through this process and not wasting money on drugs that are not going to get through in a critical area? They will also want to know how quickly can we get such products through into production and to supply. Then, finally, how are we going to launch the product and how is it going to get to market. So, you can see that all along this chain there are questions of productivity in terms of how well the money is spent and not wasted and there are questions on the quality of management at each point in terms of effectively pushing the product through the chain. Are they going to be feasible for the market place? This goes right through to the licensing process and the patenting process, etc.*

Branded goods company case

In this case the company continuously created new strategic options through gradual innovation.

We have an existing product and brand platform in areas such as disinfectants. We try to gradually innovate on this base and adapt the product to the changing preferences in the market place. This is like gradually going up a set of steps. One step at a time. We begin by finding how consumer preferences are changing, we change the product, we then find how the consumer has reacted or changed and then we change again. In this way we hope to be able to protect our brands. We also hope to protect the value they bring to the company through the intangibles associated with the brand such as the hold over the consumer's mind and their preference to buy through branded goods. We try to build a constant rate of innovation in keeping consumer interest in the brands. We are, therefore, trying to produce a step change in direct product innovation which is the main driver for growth by selling better performing, more convenient or better value products to meet consumers' needs. We do not completely try to change the brand. These are marginal or newish changes. For example, we may change the fragrance of an air freshener. This is not rocket science but we are trying to get better performance out of the existing brands that satisfy consumer needs. Another example of gradual innovation is that originally dishwashers used powder and then we moved on to tablets and now we have got the dual action tablet which both rinse and have detergent. This kind of innovation covered ten years and was quite slow. We are trying to do this over shorter periods of two or three years.

Consumer goods company case

In the following case the company created strategic options by combining old and new intangibles, stretching intangibles, and by buying new intangibles:

We are not a complex production business or a complex user of raw materials. The making of confectionery may be slightly more complex than the making of beverages, but none of this is rocket science. The real value in this business lies in the brands, the brand management end and the marketing end and that is what we have to build up and develop as our strength, our key combined intangibles to create value, and we have to make sure we fully exploit them through the beverages and the confectionery stream. This is why our strategy is all about focusing our core growth markets of beverages and confectionery. This is why it is all about developing robust, sustainable market positions which are built upon this platform of strong brand and supporting franchises. This is really about expanding our market share through innovation in the products, packaging and route to market where economically profitable. This is why our strategy is about enhancing our market positions by acquisitions or disposals. We develop new options based on existing brands, but we also seek new products within these brands, new markets for these brands, new distribution channels for these brands, and we also purchase new brands. These new options also crucially depend on our existing brand management and marketing skills. We try to combine old intangibles in new situations in old and new ways.

Valuation issues in the corporate value-creation process

In the above discussion the horizontal and network corporate value-creation processes were jointly interpreted as an option creation, waiting and exercise process. This interpretation of part of the value-creation process illustrates that the option categories can be matched to a conventional adjusted present value (APV) valuation of the company where corporate value can be interpreted as the sum of the net present values of the company base case existing operations, plus the present value of existing options, plus the present value of the process of creating them, plus the present value of top management and the board in creating extra value. Thus the asset value of the company is as shown in Diagram 5.

Diagram 5 - The asset value of a company

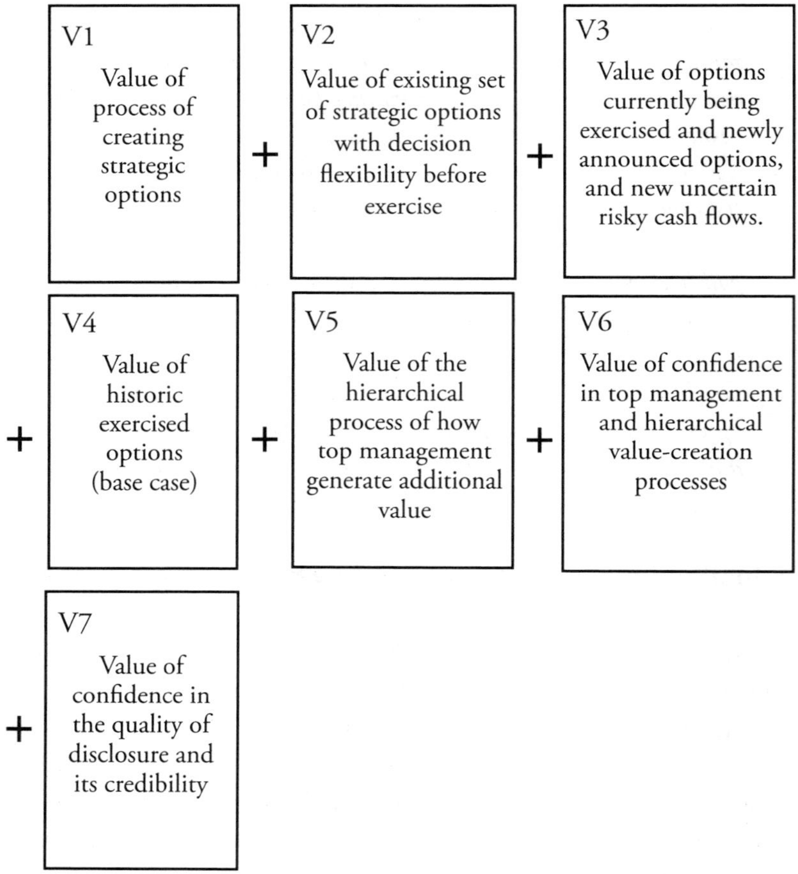

In addition asset value can also be added, through improved confidence in the market of the hierarchical value-creation process, especially the quality of top management resulting from the track record and promises that have been kept (V6). Further value can be created from increased confidence in the quality of disclosure and its credibility (V7).

The valuation equation and its seven categories summarises the dominant view of the case companies regarding the identity of the main value elements of strategic options. These are somewhat simplified categories and the actual case data involved more overlap and connections between these categories. For example, V5 is the internal management skills of top management in generating additional cash flows. These are separated from V6 on how these skills created external confidence about the company. Element V7 refers to the additional confidence that arose from the quality of external financial communication to the stock market. Each of these components were identified in the cases as critical drivers of the stock price.

V1 to V4 refer to those parts of the value-creation process that directly generate the risky cash flows and options which are the core basis for valuing the company. V4 is the base case or the present value (PV) of earnings and cash flows from the existing business operations, made up of historic exercised options. V3 is the value of transient, new cash flows and earnings derived from the recent exercise of strategic options; these earnings may or may not eventually contribute to base case earnings and cash flows. V3 and V4 could be valued using conventional discounted cash flow (DCF) methods. V2 refers to the set of unexercised growth options and these are expected to be a potential source of capital gains in the stock price once their associated cash flows are recognised. V1 values the uncertain process of creating growth through strategic options, organic growth and searching for takeover targets, and this will also be reflected in the stock price once a company has established a track record. V1 and V2 could be valued using option theory, thereby recognising that uncertainty and flexibility have value in their own right. These four present value elements are fairly conventional relative to finance theory.

However, V5, V6 and V7 were also identified in the cases as important components of value and the stock price. V5 can be interpreted as a value element which captures how top management, the board and the four hierarchical value drivers all directly influence the level of growth options, expected cash flows and their risks in V1 to V4. In the cases, the view expressed was that the higher the quality of the top team, the better their strategy, and the higher their shareholder wealth management motivation, then the better the growth options and the expected cash flows, and the lower the risk. Weaker management with poor strategies and weak motivation were expected to perform much more poorly with the same set of assets, or horizontal and network value-creation processes.

Top management, the board and the alignment of the four hierarchical value drivers were also considered to be critical sources of confidence about the company value-creation processes and the net cash flows generated; V6, therefore, showed how top management and board skills also contained a confidence component and V7 captured the way in which the quality of corporate disclosure was also a critical source of confidence about the company value-creation processes and the net cash flows generated, V6 and V7, therefore, related to confidence increases rather than cash flow increases. Both of these present value elements reflected the reduced uncertainty for the present values of V1 to V5 and were based on top management quality, corporate track record, the record of promises made and kept, and the quality of disclosure. The case data indicated that factors such as high quality management, with good track records, and high disclosure quality reputations, were likely to be related and have a cumulative effect in reducing the cost of equity capital. These value increments V6 and V7, therefore, arose from a lower equity cost of capital being used in the market to discount the expected cash flows in V1 to V5.

The next chapter explores how the case companies sought to boost understanding and confidence amongst their core fund managers and analysts. Company information about value elements V1 to V5, the cash flow changes and option value elements, were intermediated into prices *via* the understanding amongst core fund managers and analysts. Information about value elements V6 and V7, the confidence elements, were created by company track records and fund managers and analysts learning over time about V1 to V5; these in turn helped create confidence amongst core fund managers and analysts in the market for information. V6 and V7, therefore, attempt to capture or define the increment to company value created by establishing confidence amongst core fund managers and analysts.

The following pharmaceuticals and oil company cases provide more explicit illustration of the above valuation equation and interactions, especially elements V1 to V4.

Pharmaceuticals company case

> *Many of our areas of discovery and clinical development can be seen as real options, strategic options. The value of our enterprise could be a group of strategic options covering the intangibles plus the subsequent steady cash flow. To some extent, at the basic science area, it is a bit like investing in a diamond mine or a black hole in the ground. For example, we could apply the idea of an option to the discovery of drugs that might be useful, maybe three in a hundred only are discovered that we think are potentially useful. This creates choices in subsequent clinical development. From this we develop a knowledge intensive drug and from this we develop a patent and then we have the controlled cash flows and high margin which creates the high value. Once we have patents out and are producing the drugs then it should be fairly easy and predictable to value this part of the enterprise every two-year or three-year period. … Because we have the price power, the market power and, therefore, we can command high margins and know our current patents, our market share and the prices we charge,*

the earnings should be fairly predictable. These kinds of cash flows can be discounted using DCF methods in a traditional way, but they only form part of our stock price. This also creates the cash flow to feed back into long-term investments in science discovery.

The value of this company is made up of a whole set of intangible options plus known cash flows. You could ask: What is the strategic option value of target research? Of discovery? Of evaluation and clinical trials? Of clinical development and regulatory approval? Of setting up manufacturing and supply? Of managing our patents? or put these questions another way: What does basic science produce? What does discovery produce and how do we get suitable candidates for evaluation? How do we start the early clinical trials and what is the success rate there? Then, what is the value of clinical development and regulatory approval? How good are we at testing products and not wasting money. Then what is the value of setting up manufacturing and supply? and finally, what is the value of managing our patents and getting our patents lined up at the right time so that we have a regular supply of patents?

Now all of these are uncertain and they require special management skills … They all give us an opportunity to create delayed value in the future and we can make choices about this. This is clearly classic strategic option valuation.

Oil company case

This company is made up of a set of strategic options. We have oil in the ground which we own and it can get out whenever we want. We have also got drilling rights and rights to explore and licences to produce and, again, this is a major source of cash flows. We have the ability to find oil and then we have got the ability to bid for drilling rights. Some of these advantages lead to cash flows immediately. Oil in the ground is a licence to print money.

We can get a steady set of cash flows depending upon the oil price, which is the only major variable here. We can discount the cash flows here easily. The discovery, drilling and other advantages create strategic options and allow us choices and flexibility in the future as to whether to expand or delay production and make more money here. You value this using strategic option analysis.

Cash flows at points in the value-creation process

The case companies indicated that cash flows were invested and generated at each key phase in the internal value-creation process. In aggregate net form, these created stable and transient cash flows to be divided between security holders, bondholders and shareholders, and internal reinvestment. The latter became a key cash flow input to the continuous option creation and use process and so the cycle continued. Brealey and Myers (2003) categorise the key cash flows in the firm as follows:

1 Cash raised from investors – equity and debt.

2 Cash invested in the firm

3 Cash generated by operations

4a Cash re-invested – internal equity

4b Cash returned to investors – dividends, share repurchase, debt capital and interest repayments

In the case companies these key cash flows can be associated with the value elements in the adjusted present value equation.

Diagram 6 - The cash flows of a company

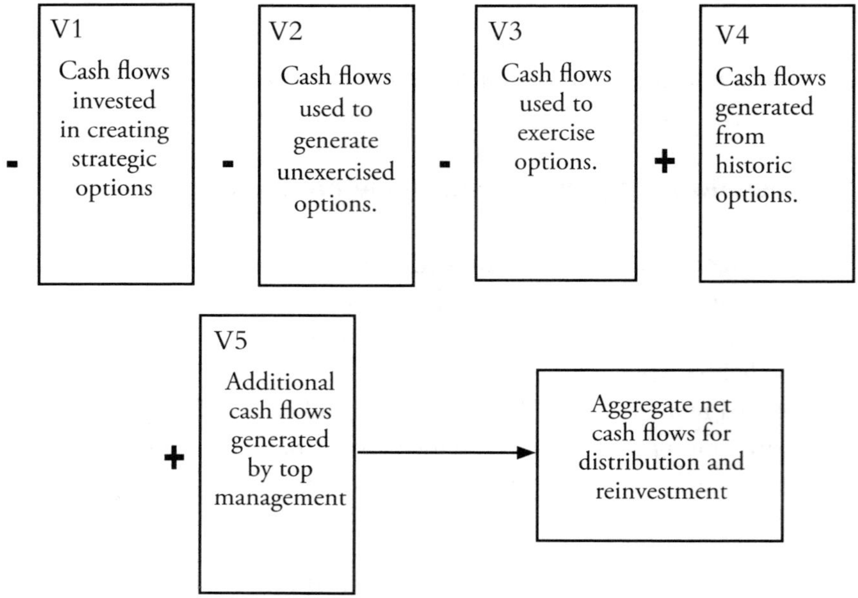

The above cash flow analysis does not include the uncertainty arising from these options.

In this study analysts were constantly seeking information on cash flows which broadly corresponded to the cash flow categories shown above. The case companies were more cautious about releasing such precise cash flow information because of the price-sensitive information implications. However, the following quotes reveal that the firms released some cash flow information as part of their value-creation story; this was likely to be about major categories of sources and use of cash flows rather than about levels or changes. Information on cash flow levels was released through the financial statements, while news of significant changes had to be released as price-sensitive information. However, the case companies perceived that analysts and fund managers were using an active dialogue with the case companies on the publicly known value-creation story to develop additional insights into company cash flow behaviour.

Practical examples of cash flow information in the option process.

The following cases cover four different sectors and illustrate how cash flows at various phases in the option use and creation process were released through the value-creation story. This feature of the story was important in creating an informed context to explain other cash flow information released in the public domain.

Tobacco company case

The real added value lies in our cigarette brands: These are the real intangibles that count in this business. There are other important intangibles such as the quality of the distribution system. These are at the marketing end as well and they are very important in this business. In terms of brands we did a DCF analysis of brands last year. We have projected the cash flows arising from these brands over the next few years. On this basis you would expect the share price to be about twelve pounds. In reality it is only four pounds at present. Why is there such a big difference? This is the litigation effect; the possibility of litigation and the size of the award are, themselves, intangibles. Litigation is obscuring the value that arises out of our brands and the steady high quality cash flow they produce. Other factors such as market sentiment are also pulling down our price. To some extent the company is falling out of fashion. The greatest intangibles really are our brands and the cash flow generative powers they have. However, these brands are not on the balance sheet. This seems odd because our international brands are the key to growth in the cigarette business. The domestic brands are not normally a source of growth, but they are a source of very stable cash flows in certain economies. For example, we have a strong brand in Canada and this has a very high market share and high margins. This is a very good steady cash flow and a valuable brand. The point about international brands is that they are brands that get you established, especially in the higher value, higher margin tobacco products. They allow us to break into new markets and to generate new risky cash flows which is our source of growth value. Success in managing these brands is a key intangible. We are trying to move up from lower margin tobacco products to higher brand classes and, therefore, increase the certainty and size of the cash flows that arise from these businesses. This clearly is very helpful if there is any downturn in the demand for cigarette smoking. We can improve the size of our cash flows and their quality at the same time as reducing volume. Obviously, value would increase under these circumstances, not decline, as brand management is a key intangible which, if we get it right, can add value to the enterprise quite a bit. We have done extensive brand valuations here and DCF analysis of brands. We have found recently that some of the domestic brands are the most valuable brands. For example, I have mentioned in Canada we have XXXX (a very high) per cent of the market with the FFFFFF brand. In fact, in our discounted cash flow analysis of valuation we find that the top four domestic brands are worth more than the current share price capitalisation of the company. This shows how much the litigation in the US is having an effect on our share price.

Insurance company case

Traditional skills or intangibles in this business are to do with underwriting and claims management. We are trying to improve the management of our claims management. As an industry we spend many billions per year settling non-life claims and we are now exploiting our purchasing power in buying replacement goods. We are also cracking down on fraud. We can quantify this improvement in our claims management as saving over £10 million per year. We will probably save more as we introduce Internet ordering. Customers will benefit from seven-day delivery installation and security marking and we will benefit by lower costs. Further savings will come from a tougher drive against fraudulent claims - especially household claims - and we expect a worldwide fraud reduction target in excess of £50 million. So this is a very practical way of reducing the volatility on our return on capital.

Branded goods company case

This is a company where the brands are the key intangibles. We spend a lot of money on market research and try to find out what consumer preferences are and what the competition is doing. We do not have laboratories, we are not that kind of rocket science company. We spend a lot of money advertising in the media for all of our products to keep up product awareness ... Our brands are important ways for creating value in our drinks and confectionery businesses. Brands are like a contract with consumers to produce regular cash flows. They are the foundation on which we can build new products and create new choices for the company in terms of its product range. This is a valuable strategic option and we spend a lot of money maintaining the master brands and building on these.

Chemical company case

Basic questions are being asked all along our value chain, in each individual business and in terms of the connections between these businesses. Fundamental questions are being asked at the financial facts end and its connection to our story about value creation. So, for example, questions are being asked about whether cash flows are being eaten up by the restructuring costs as the company moves away from bulk chemicals to speciality chemicals. Questions are being asked as to whether the debt levels are too high as a result of the WWWW speciality chemicals purchase and how is the company going to release this. In other words, is the company going to be so cash strapped that it won't be able to deal with the problems of connecting together these different value chains and growing these chains.

Retail company case in alliance with a bank

The following case reveals how the story was used to reveal information about cash flows derived from alliances with other companies:

We have a joint venture with XXXX bank whereby we offer their banking services under our brand name in our stores. We get the chance to stretch our brand for food and clothes retailing into financial services. This has improved the cash flows generated by this intangible and increased its value and the value of our shares. The bank gets the extra banking business and better economies of scale in its back office banking operations. This improves their margins and cash flows. We both win.

Value-relevant information

The information asymmetry between the companies and external suppliers of capital fund managers and analysts related to the joint nature of the corporate value-creation process and company cash flows.

The present value elements in the adjusted present value equation provide a clear valuation focus for company disclosures. Changes in these elements were likely to have information content for stock prices. Information on cash flow levels at each key phase in the value-creation story, or in each equivalent PV element in the APV equation, was perceived to provide analysts and fund managers with fundamental information for valuation.

In the cases, internal value-creation cash flows were netted out [as investment (-ve) and as newly generated cash flows (+ve)] and aggregated. These summary cash flows were normally reported in financial statements, but the detailed cash flows were not. The summary cash flows formed the stable and transient cash flows to be divided between external security holders and internal re-investment. The latter was a key cash flow input to the continuous option creation and use process in the case companies. If the funds required for reinvestment were greater than those from retained earnings, then the case companies had to seek finance in external markets.

Changes in cash flows in each external-internal cash flow category were likely to be value-relevant for the case companies. Information, such as on the broad scale of their internal investment needs and their cash generation capability, was likely to be released as public disclosure by companies. This information was also signalled through profitability changes and by observable alterations to share repurchases, new issues, dividends and capital structure.

The case companies recognised that markets used relevant information, whatever its source, to make inferences about cash flow levels and changes. They perceived that cash flow changes could also be deduced and checked by fund managers and analysts from private and public disclosure of changes in the value-creation story and that cash flows and changes could be deduced from corporate signals relating to dividends and capital structure. The latter provided a check on the story; as a result the case firms used a mixture of these approaches to disclose new information about cash flow levels and changes.

Role of valuation models

In terms of the above valuation equation, the case managers associated conventional valuation models such as price-earnings (P:E) ratios and detailed cash flows with valuation of base case and exercised options. In contrast, unexercised options were regarded as 'fudge factors' rather than formal option models. For example, V2 value was concerned with growth beyond the intermediate horizon and involved 'blue sky' valuations or 'fudge' valuations by analysts and fund managers whereby 'adjustments' were made to the conventional valuation models based on qualitative information. The problems of using formal valuation models was briefly mentioned in the cases as demonstrated by the following two cases.

Bank case

> *Using NPV to value these options is misleading given that they are options and not well understood investment projects. We therefore try to be more imaginative in our assessment of how value might be created here, and we accept they may appear to be negative NPV at the start.*

Pharmaceuticals company case

> *We know that one of our competitors, XXX, has considered employing formal option valuation models to our type of business. We have yet to do this because we cannot see where the data is going to come from. The estimates are very dodgy and we think it best to use the option idea to understand what is going on.*

The bulk of the case companies did not use the formal language of financial or strategic options to describe or value these choices; they also tended not to employ real option concepts or valuation methods. Five case companies used the language of strategic options to discuss how they developed valuable strategic flexibility and choices. Three R&D intensive cases and one innovative bank mentioned the potential for using formal valuation models, with one of these companies noting that its main competitor used such an approach. In the bulk of cases, the companies used concepts concerning the creation and use of strategic flexibility; they were aware of which option-like variables were important to the valuation of their strategic flexibility, without referring to option language or terms to describe them. The companies used their practical concepts of strategic flexibility to define categories of value-relevant information which were similar to those identified in the above analysis.

Kobrak and Spieser (2000) identify similar problems to the above case companies regarding the use of option theory in valuing corporate flexibility. In particular, the authors recognise the problems of identifying and measuring "time to expiry" and competitor reaction in determining the underlying asset and estimating its volatility. These problems, they argue, limit the use of formal option theory, and leave companies with little choice but to revert back to conventional analysis. Busby and Pitts (1997) surveyed FTSE 100 companies and found that only four UK finance directors had heard of the use of option theory to value strategic options. The combination of real problems of implementation, and of ignorance of the approach, may prove to be a major barrier to the full use of formal option theory. This may, in turn, explain the case companies' desire to use more practical concepts of 'flexibility' and 'strategic options' when disclosing information in the company value-creation story.

Company disclosure and value-relevant information

Internal value-creation cash flow data was an important data element for case company valuation. However, in a present value model additional discount rate information is required from capital markets to formally value the present value elements (V4). In the option valuation model, additional information on exercise price, value of the underlying asset, volatility and other factors are required to formally value the present value elements (V1, V2) (Brealey and Myers, 2003).

Hence, a mixture of company-supplied and market-supplied information was required to value each element of the adjusted present value equation. Some data such as discount rates could be measured. However, much of the valuation data had to be based on estimates.

These estimates and subsequent company valuations in the market were perceived to depend upon a wider understanding and confidence amongst core fund managers and analysts (see Chapter 5). Corporate disclosure of the story of the value-creation process and on broad cash flow categories helped create this confidence and understanding.

The following categories of information were perceived by the case companies as being *ex-ante* value relevant for analysts and fund managers. The categories have been matched to the valuation categories in the adjusted present value model. They contributed stable structure to the value-creation story.

- V1 strategic options was concerned with valuing the uncertain process of creating growth through generating strategic options (organic growth and searching for takeover targets), over a long term horizon. Information was disclosed about expenditure on R&D, on developing brands, staff, and processes, and about general success in creating options. The case companies released information *via* the value-creation story to provide an informed context or wider picture for fund managers and analysts to interpret changing events.
- V2 options related to growth beyond the two-year to three-year operating horizon; and focused on how new sources of additional value in the company were created by the creation of new exercisable options. V2 disclosure concerned story information about the broad nature of product market options or the competitive flexibility that the company was creating; this included information about the next major class of projects or options the company was expected to be

involved in. The details were not released because these were still concepts or unexercised options rather than actual action. Broad narrative information was released about the timing of these options such as how the company waited until it learnt about the best external market conditions or best state of the internal value-creation process. The companies also discussed the difference between the 'experimental exercise and testing of ideas' *versus* 'well-understood option exercise'. The case companies also released a lot of contextual information *via* the value-creation story and benchmarks.

- V3 exercise of new options involved the value of new, transient cash flows and earnings derived from the recent exercise of strategic options. Value-relevant information about V3 involved disclosure announcements about the exercise of the new options and subsequent disclosure about recent progress. It also included specific information about new products, use of brands and new flexible uses of production as well as disclosure about problems and successes. The case companies released full details about exercised options through stock exchange announcements, as well as by their observed actions. Care was taken with price-sensitive information and public announcements.
- V4 current operations was the value arising from current operations, current trading and immediate growth. The valuation horizon was quite short, at about two or three years and was based on historically exercised options which had matured. Value-relevant information about V4 was based on information about the existing business such as progress and current trading performance; it also concerned the way in which cash flows were generated and consumed in the existing business, information about potentially abandoning businesses and project successes/failures over time. The case companies released continuous details on the base case through periodic reporting and announcements, as well as by their observed actions.

- V5 top management value-relevant information related to the issue of how top management, the board and the four value-drivers all directly influenced the level of expected cash flows and their risks in value elements V1 to V4.
- V6 confidence boosting value-relevant information also included information on top management, the board and the alignment of the four value hierarchical drivers which boosted confidence about the company value-creation processes and the net cash flows generated in V1 to V5 above. V6 confidence information included a track record of keeping strategic and financial performance promises over a long period of time. V6 information was often based on involuntary disclosure or external observation of how effective top management actions had been, and how effective historic execution of promises had been.
- V7 corporate disclosure which captured how the quality of corporate disclosure also acted as a critical source of confidence about the company value-creation processes and the net cash flows generated. V6 information concerned external observation of how credible and trustworthy the content of corporate disclosure had been. Disclosure and observation about V1 to V5 provided benchmark information to check promises and create track records for both V6 and V7. The V7 information category differed from the V6 element in that it referred to disclosure quality *per se* and not to the top management team that produced it. Clearly there was some overlap between these categories.

The above information categories reveal that the case companies tried to deal with a key dilemma, *ie.* they did not desire the release of details concerning the V1 and V2 processes, but they did wish to signal that these processes existed. The firms wanted to reveal that they had a reserve of extra information about the efficiency of the corporate economic transformation process and to signal that the processes eventually led to success and that disclosure about V1 to V4 was credible.

The following two examples reveal how the cases had to pursue this disclosure policy over a long time period.

Bank case

> *In the case of implementing options, you have to be in it for the long run and you have to learn to ride short term price fluctuations or even reductions as the market tries to understand what the new strategic option is and how we are exploiting it. The joint venture with XXXX is one example. Our price fell once we announced it and it took some time before the market understood how we were getting so many new customers and how the joint venture was not hurting our brand or market share.*

Pharmaceutical company case

> *In terms of the analysts and the fund managers, we do explain a lot about R&D and the technical side to these people. Many of them are fairly competent in the situation. They have a good background in this field. So we will spend a lot of time talking about R&D, product testing, patents and the immediate product pipeline.*

By identifying the seven information categories above, the case companies were able to continuously signal value-relevant information and to know exactly why they were releasing such information. All of these signals fit within the 'pecking order' disclosure model discussed in chapter three. V3, V4 and V5 signals were primarily released *via* public and private channels. V1 and V2 were released *via* private channels using informal mechanisms such as the value-creation story. All signals were subject to secrecy, but the secrecy pressures and constraints operated most strongly on categories V1 and V2; V6 and V7 information was 'released' by observation in private and in public.

The next chapter investigates how the above came to form part of the dynamic feedback process whereby continuous company disclosure created market understanding about company value creation (horizontal and network). This understanding, coupled with the further release of information over time about the quality of both top management (V6) and corporate disclosure (V7), created the conditions for confidence in the company's future prospects. These will be explored in chapter five.

Summary

This chapter has outlined the key elements of the model of financial communications whereby the story of value creation and the use of benchmarks were used together to communicate fragmented and qualitative information about the role of intangibles in corporate value creation. The chapter employed major theoretical constructs to interpret the story of value creation, to value the value-creation story elements, and to identify *ex-ante* value-relevant information at the heart of financial communications. These concepts included ideas of: valuing strategic options; a continuous option creation and exercise process; using the adjusted present value model to value elements of the option process; and identifying relevant cash flow categories.

The case data has also revealed how 'good practice' in financial communications can be based on a combination of the case insights and the application of relevant corporate finance theory including an option perspective. The case company concepts of strategic flexibility (development and use) matched a broader model of strategic option creation and exercise. The broader conceptual framework embodied in options valuation, when combined with adjusted present value concepts and cash flow categories from corporate finance theory, provide a clear language to discuss and articulate the seven primary value-relevant information categories identified in the case data. Clear guidance can therefore be provided to management regarding what are likely to be broad categories of information for disclosure in their financial communications with the stock market especially within their narrative or story of value creation.

Chapter Five

Corporate Perceptions of Fund Manager and Analyst Learning, of Barriers to Learning and of Fragility

Chapter five describes the interaction between the companies and information and stock markets, and outlines how this learning process informed analysts and fund managers. The chapter also discusses the nature of the perceived learning arising in these markets, the barriers to interaction and learning, the fragility of this knowledge and the broad nature of feedback from the markets.

The case companies perceived that their financial communications using their story and benchmark information changed fund managers and analysts 'understanding and confidence', and these in turn impacted on the stock market. The interaction involved cumulative two-way learning by fund managers, analysts, traders and company managers. Growing shareholder wealth pressures from private meetings - buttressed by continuous and cumulative feedback from market prices - created an important context, or atmosphere, for such private interactions. Diagram 7 summarises this interaction.

Diagram 7 - Corporate and market interaction

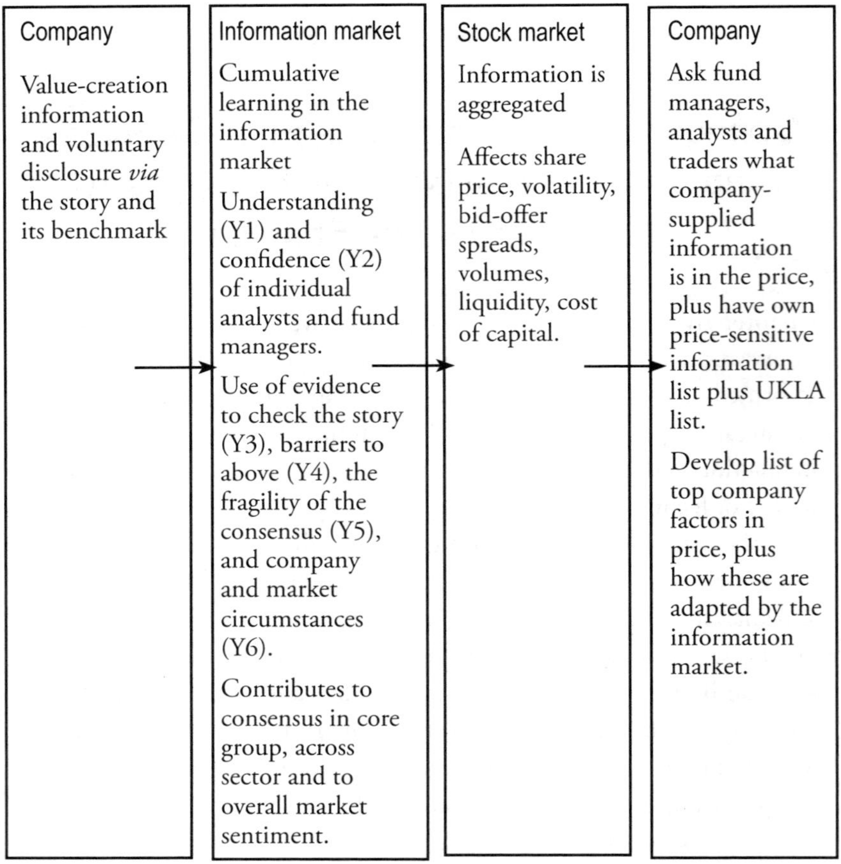

The company value-creation story created understanding and confidence in corporate disclosures. These were the outcome, in part, of a fund managers' and analysts' processes of using concrete and subjective evidence, company and external, to test the company story and to check promises. The market outcome resulted in a consensus of a core group of key fund managers and analysts about company's expected financial earnings numbers and about value-creation stories. Major barriers and problems were observed in the evidence-collection and checking process. The case companies expended time and financial resources to probe and receive feedback on what information was in the information-market amongst fund managers and analysts. The understanding and confidence amongst fund managers and analysts were perceived as acting as informed contexts for understanding new information or events, and were viewed as playing a central role in valuation. However, this confidence was very fragile with respect to company surprises and to changes in market sentiment. This fragility was due in part to natural business exposures to business risk as well as poor corporate track records. Fragility was also due to high financial communications exposures where the company was always a focus of the financial media, any other media and the public interest. The fragility of this understanding and confidence was perceived to contribute to equivalent fragility in earnings estimates and valuations.

The companies perceived that fund managers and analysts played a critical role in intermediating this company specific information into stock prices and into their share price volatility, liquidity, bid-offer spread, and cost of capital. The case companies expended time and financial resources to probe and receive feedback on what company disclosures were in the stock price. Sudden or gradual changes in stock market prices were often the first observable feedback signal that problems or opportunities were being recognised by the market in the execution of the corporate value-creation story and in disclosure behaviour. As a result, the stock market reaction to corporate disclosure, as well as general sector and stock market movements, was continuously and closely monitored by the case companies. Fund managers and analysts further amplified this stock market feedback by their comments during these private interactions.

The case companies expected that the stock market would build in or discount the information-markets confidence in corporate disclosure behaviour. This cost of equity capital 'information premium' was expected to remain stable relative to competitors with lower quality disclosure. Unexpected deviations from this expectation benchmark were expected to impact on prices and other stock market attributes. A similar cost of equity capital premium was also identified for factors associated with top management qualities and with the effectiveness of the wider hierarchical value-creation process. In this context, high fragility could also be interpreted as creating a more variable equity cost of capital.

The interactions and the dialogue

A key part of top management's role (chairman, chief executive, finance director, and investor relations staff) lay in regular private communication through one-to-one meetings and telephone calls with major fund managers and core analysts. These private disclosure interactions were driven by many factors including the financial reporting cycle, as well as *ad hoc* events (Holland, 1997) as demonstrated in the case below:

Property company case

> *Also, in terms of disclosure effectiveness, we see the top thirty fund managers per annum for the one-on-ones. We may see the next twenty or so every two or three years and we may also see another ten fund managers who do not hold our stock for one-on-ones within a year. We do the latter because we may wish to persuade them to come on our shareholder base. This is often American fund managers who want to also find out about the property market and use us as a reference point.*

Marston and Empson (2004) found that in an average year, companies held five general meetings and 77 one-to-one meetings. The mean number of site visits was 3.8 and the mean number of roadshows was 4.8. The one-to-one meetings typically involved the chief executive and/or the chief finance officer with members of the investor relations team, and these met an equivalent fund manager or analyst team. These figures indicate a large increase in the number of meetings since 1991, when the UK's top 500 companies were reported as holding an average of 25 one-to-one meetings (Marston, 1993). The UK data can also be compared with a 2002 survey revealing a mean number of one-to-one meetings of 112 for the European top 500 (Marston, 2004). The European respondents were larger, in terms of market capitalisation, than the UK respondents and this may partly explain the difference.

Creating high quality interaction with fund managers and analysts was a major priority for the case companies as shown in the following case.

Bank case

> *At present I would say the main problem with the analysts is getting their interest and this is a barrier to their understanding of the key intangibles in this business. ... We need to establish a regular dialogue with the serious influencers in the market. Once you can do this you can develop a dialogue and build up their interest over time and build up your reputation for more open communication. Once you develop this base of interest in the company you can then make the dialogue more complicated and they will naturally start asking you deeper questions as they learn more about the company. It is from this more informed base that you can communicate the difficult qualitative information such as how you are dealing with these new kinds of banking channels, demonstrating how good you are at designing new products and at adapting existing products. You can show them how much you can learn from one set of products and transfer them to another. It is this kind of thing that you can get over once you have got them interested.*

The key point of interaction occurred between elite corporate management and senior fund managers. These parties tended to share many common values about the functions of enterprise and finance. The top management and board members of the companies were both members of their own company and of the external world of finance located in the City of London; to some extent they recognised that they had to reflect the values, norms, language, and concepts of this world and to intermediate these to middle management and employees.

Company management and the fund managers shared a common uncertain future about the effective corporate use of capital and fund managers' use of scarce top management skills; they could not observe each other's actions all of the time. In a world of uncertainty there was a clear limit to formal, or 'black letter', contracting to fully specify their economic relationships and, as a result, they tended to use ideas of implicit contracting, or of 'relations' of trust and confidence, to characterise their interactions and economic relationships (Holland, 1995).

The case companies also identified 'atmosphere' as an important context for their regular interactions with fund managers. For example, growing shareholder wealth pressures from private meetings, buttressed by continuous and cumulative feedback from market prices, created an important context or atmosphere for such private disclosure interactions. The 'atmosphere' was normally future orientated, dealing with issues of vision, the direction the company wished to go, and the 'big picture'. However, the 'atmosphere' could vary along dimensions from an open, co-operative two-way dialogue with high trust, to a 'frozen', 'chilled', antagonistic and one-way low trust atmosphere. The latter was unusual, and was caused by corporate specific problems such as an unexpected financing needs, poor financial performance and other crisis as well as by market-wide effects, for example, the new UK PSI guidance in 1994 and the SEC 'Fair Disclosure' rules of 2000.

The companies perceived that core fund managers used the relationship and the meetings' 'atmosphere' to influence their behaviour. The core fund managers tried to persuade the case companies to internalise shareholder wealth management aims in the corporate value-creation processes and in disclosure. In particular, they attempted to influence the shareholder wealth management content of: *(i)* the story and benchmarks; *(ii)* other public and private disclosure; and *(iii)* the corporate balance between secrecy and disclosure and can be interpreted as fund managers using social means to toughen the terms of the 'softer' less explicit 'relationship' contract.

Perceived understanding and confidence amongst fund managers and analysts

The interaction involved a continuous and cumulative two-way learning process by fund managers, analysts, and company managers as illustrated in Diagram 8.

Diagram 8: Two-way learning process

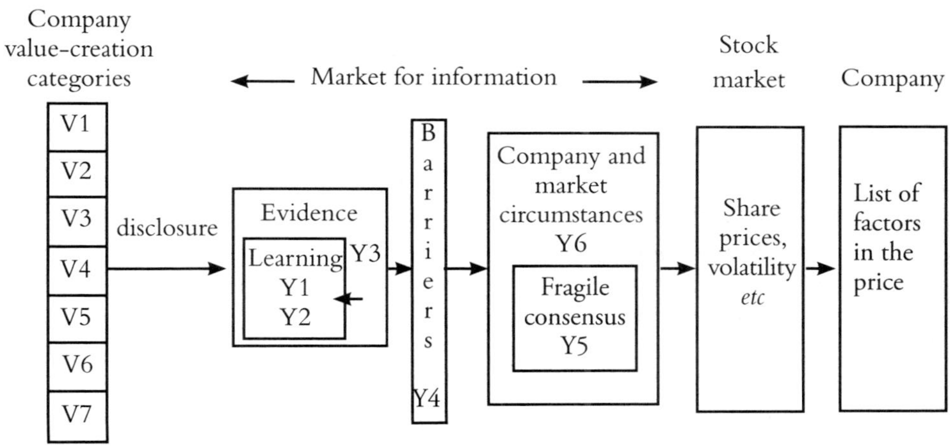

The case companies perceived that their interaction created understanding (Y1), and confidence (Y2) within individual key analysts and core fund managers. These were perceived to be aggregated into an equivalent consensus amongst the group of core fund managers and analysts as well as in the wider market for information, and were manifest as numeric and qualitative information (see later in this chapter and chapter six for details).

Y1: Perceived understanding amongst fund managers and analysts

The company view of fund managers' or analysts' understanding was based on a perception of the information needs arising out of common elements of a fund manager's portfolio decisions, as well as common elements of an analyst's stock and sector decision as demonstrated in the following two cases:

Bank case

> *... the fund managers make judgements about our story of technology and branch infrastructure, and the combined package of management quality, strategy and technology. They make judgements as to which companies have the right combination of this package ... They see many companies and they find it easy to understand the important aspects of value and they spend a lot of time trying to get a grip on management quality. The fund managers can distinguish between the management qualities of different companies.*

Oil company case

> *... fund managers do not have a lot of time to come and see us and we need to get our message across quickly with clarity and, therefore, this is a means to influence the way in which the fund managers think about us. We want them to understand how the company is different to other oil companies and similar companies and, therefore, they can invest in the company. We therefore try*

and give them a reason to put another pound into us rather than YYY.

Top management quality was perceived to be a very important component of analyst's and fund manager's understanding of the company. The following quote shows how information about top management quality was disclosed or observed. The comments also indicate that this information mainly concerned the way in which these qualities played a role in producing incremental returns in terms of extra cash flows and earnings.

Insurance company case

The fund managers are assessing if our chief executive has good people around him. They are seeing if he has got a good team, if he can delegate. They want to know if he can take the tough decisions and whether there is going to be blood on the carpet in terms of getting rid of more salesmen ... They want to see if he is a strategic thinker and whether he can actually implement the strategy and show he can implement it. They want to be sure that he is not emotionally tied to some of the businesses or strategic business units identified above. They also want the chief executive to make explicit the target of return. They want to hear what it's going to be for each of these key strategic business units and, of course, we must achieve it as individual businesses, and overall. Otherwise, promises are just not good enough. The quality of the top management group of chief executive and the finance director in particular is pretty critical. Fund managers are betting that the top management group will increase the consensus down through the middle management and through the chief executives of the strategic business units. They are betting on the qualities of top management in increasing the value created in the strategic business units identified above. They wish to see if top management and its strategy are creating a common sense of purpose throughout the organisation and creating a glue for the whole business across all these strategic business activities. They, therefore, want to know if the top management can drive the decision strategy and vision down into the strategic business units. The chief executive needs to demonstrate that this is the case in the large business.

The following quote also shows how information on top management quality was used to identify the extent to which top management produced incremental cash flows and earnings; it also shows how this strategic execution skill was different from financial communication skills.

Technology company case

I think fund managers find it easy to spot top management stars because they stand out in terms of their track record and their strategy. They can pick out stars such as communicators and performers because they do stand out. The question is, can they find the average performer and can they distinguish the vast bulk of top management? They are also trying to assess whether management are seeking control of the market, by trying to achieve price power or margin power. These are critical variables that they are trying to assess. Again, all of these intangibles can only be assessed by direct contact and direct dialogue. However, they can be fooled by some top management individuals who are just good presenters. These individuals may not be very good at executing strategy. Sometimes fund managers cannot separate these two qualities of communication skills and of execution skills. They have to wait until the track record emerges and then they can check whether the vision matches the execution.

The increasing value significance of top management financial communication skills in enhancing understanding and confidence for UK companies is revealed by Marston and Empson (2004). They noted that almost half of chief executives devoted more than 10% of their time to investor relations and that 70% were allocating more time than they had been three years before.

Y2: Perceived confidence amongst fund managers and analysts

This learning and understanding (Y1) also played a role in boosting individual analyst's and fund manager's confidence (Y2) in the company value-creation story. These were derived from involuntary disclosure or external observation of how credible and trustworthy corporate disclosure and effectiveness had been, and how effective historic execution of promises had been. These sources were also intermediated in stock prices and were expected to reduce the cost of equity capital and generate additional company value as shown in the following cases:

Oil company case

The package of intangibles and promises together create a climate of confidence around the other sources of value. They create confidence around how the existing intangibles create value now and it creates confidence around how they are expected to create it in the future. But this confidence is fragile, given the information about intangibles. There is some kind of act of faith on the part of the fund managers that these intangibles exist and contribute to value. If you like, this confidence issue may be another component of value. It may be possible to value it in the way that loan commitments are valued by banks.

Branded goods company case

You can consider the numbers in the market as consisting of two types. One, the targets we set for the year ahead and couple of years ahead and secondly the analysts' estimates of earnings and value. Both of these sets of numbers are about the future, they are uncertain. You can add to the layers of confidence surrounding these numbers. These layers could be: one, the very fact that a company has made explicit its target numbers. This can simplify the estimation process for the analysts. The fact that we are heading to exceed a certain target or achieve a certain target, certainly simplifies the job for the analysts and gives them more confidence in our numbers. Another layer of confidence around it has to do with these top management qualities and our strategy. A third layer has to do with the quality of our long-term relationships with the brokers' analysts and fund managers. If we have established trust and confidence here through a good track record over time then this gives further confidence in these targets and in the estimated numbers set out by the analysts. This also creates further confidence in our strategies and immediate plans. All of these three factors act as layers of confidence around the consensus numbers forecast by the analysts and critical intangibles in our share price.

A key factor in confidence arose on the company side. It involved the scale of unknown or invisible in the corporate value-creation chain; the higher these unknowns (low Y1) then the lower the confidence (Y2). This encouraged fund managers and analysts to use easily observable factors such as management quality to act as proxies for the unknown; it also encouraged them to use a range of methods to infer the existence of the invisibles, as demonstrated in the following case.

Consumer goods company case

Clearly, the cluster of human skills, competencies in brand management and brand effectiveness are not easily measured or understood. You really only understand them when one of the elements goes badly wrong and fund managers and analysts only really understand them when the eventual profit and loss arrives and they see the positive or negative results. This is true both of the brand management skills or in terms of training people to be winners and to have passion for winning.

Technology company case

The existence of invisibles was also inferred over time, helping to develop confidence:

> *There is a repetitive process as fund managers and analysts learn about the links between observed outputs, observed and inferred inputs, and about the invisible processes in between. In our case the inputs would be technical competence, which cannot be observed by the analysts and fund managers. They eventually see a track record of profit increase, sales increase, costs going down and product quality going up; this can be observed. This feeds back to the things that they cannot observe in terms of the technical competence in our value-creation process. What they do then is start believing the story about our competence. This occurs over many, many periods and increases their confidence in our story. So, you have this problem that many of the intangibles are not observable or are difficult to measure. The fund managers and analysts have to collect information about many intangibles, sift the evidence and then make this leap of faith in terms of connecting the story about, in our case, technical competence and its connection to financial output. A company can do very well through many scenarios. So, for example, the company can have a particular strategy that it argues fits a particular environment and over many periods there is subsequent good financial performance. In other words, the story and strategy fits the environment and eventually produces the financial performance. This builds up confidence and credibility over time.*

Top management qualities were often used as a proxy for both understanding company value-creation processes and for boosting confidence. They were also used as a research short cut when the fund managers and analysts needed to make quick decisions. For example:

Insurance company case

> *There are not many observable and concrete processes and products here. There is not a great news flow from this insurance and pension fund business. There are not many dramatic events here except the recent event of VVVV for us. This means the chief executive and the other board members and an explanation of our strategy by these people is very important. When you have many invisibles in the business and you are a low profile and low news business then this communication about top management becomes very important.*

Retail company case

> *The brokers' analysts and the fund managers do not necessarily articulate these links between intangibles, tangibles and financial affects. They do not formally model these. They can, in fact, use their view of management confidence and credibility as a short cut; if they believe the story we are talking about and it makes sense relative to the competition then they will use this to tweak their P:E relatives and be more optimistic in them. In other words, they will miss out the intervening logic about value creation and go straight to their P:E models and this is how many of these intangibles do get into the share price through such valuation.*

However, the quality of top management was a critical factor in understanding and confidence, irrespective of the issues of 'visibility' or short cuts.

Utility company case

The strategic story must explain what it is the management can do to give the fund managers some investment confidence that the strategy will be realised. Fund managers back teams, management teams and ideas with their funds when they think the story makes sense and … when management is seen to be of the highest quality and distinguishable from competitors, and are likely to win. It is these factors above all, the story, the management quality, the strategy, the implementation and execution of strategy that all play a key role in confidence and price.

Y3: Collecting evidence and the development of track records

The case companies also observed how fund managers and analysts made use of concrete evidence, company-supplied information as well as external sources, to test and corroborate the components of the corporate value-creation story, and to both check corporate promises and ask more questions of the company. This process (Y3) was the perceived means by which company information played a role in generating current fund manager and analyst understanding and confidence, as well as adding to these over time by building a corporate history or track record of story, promises, action and performance.

Property company case company

… most of the one-on-ones with the fund managers are question and answer. They know us very well and they have learnt about us over time and they know our strategy very well. Strategy is central in these meetings and it is essential that it is performance driven and that we can demonstrate that we have the means to improve our performance. Last year's promises are critical and what we said last year is thrown in our face all the time. Essentially, they

are trying to look at the whites of our eyes and ask the question, do they believe the story we are telling them about valuation creation? By this I mean the story about how we acquire assets and develop them and improve them then rent them out. How have we improved assets with existing tenants and used that as a manoeuvre to improve the rentals. They may probe us in detail on our City and West End properties which they are familiar with … They want to know, have we delivered in the past. We have. And when we do this it improves our credibility. However, it is a very difficult story to sell when you are facing a world where there are property companies in the fund managers' own portfolios doing well, without any active management, and with this tax advantage that the property companies have within the fund managers' portfolios.

The evidence-checking process used comparisons with competitors as an important reference point. The fund managers and analysts also used comparative benchmarks to check out the company story.

Technology company case

In many cases the fund managers find relative information. Because they talk to many companies in the same sector or similar sectors and they talk to the competitors, they can, therefore, uniquely gather ideas across companies and assess what is known about the value-creation process in the industry. They may, therefore, get a unique perspective relative to the top management in one company and they may be able to relatively measure the qualities of managers. However, they will never know these matters in as much depth as any manager. So the full set of information about value creation - or what top management know about value creation - they can never pursue this in depth. They can only get this relative, comparative information and this is all they really need for valuation, as far as they are concerned anyway.

Utility company case

FFFF utility has a very similar story to us but with a stronger emphasis on its infrastructure and its customer base. The brokers' analysts and the fund managers are now looking to see which of these companies has the winning execution of this story; in other words, they both have very sound and solid stories. At present it appears that we are very much better at persuading the stock market, fund managers and analysts that our story makes sense and, therefore, it has a very much higher price and P:E ratio. However, as I say, the market is watching very carefully the similar story and seeing whether there is any difference in execution and seeing who is going to be the winner.

Consumer goods company case

In the United States the beverages companies such as NNNN and MMMM and us all publish detailed sales figures and so you can figure out in this market which brand, which marketing strategy is winning best. In the United Kingdom the analysts have to dig it out of the bowels of the financial report and published information. However, in both cases they can, effectively, benchmark brand effectiveness and changes here, and when they observe this they report it and it does affect the share price.

The history or track record were also a critical point at which new meetings began, and were a key base from which case companies could explain major changes in the company story. The absence of a track record or history was recognised as a major barrier for privatised companies new to the stock market. The history was seen as the key point at which the evidence sifting and analysis process began for fund managers and analysts.

Utility company case

> *In the period 1990 to 1997 we were very much focusing on the tangibles in our business as a generator that delivers the electricity down the wires. We produced the concrete output in terms of electricity and this produced fairly clear-cut cash flows; this had the main impact on the share price. This is a highly regulated business both in terms of output and in terms of prices and, hence, in terms of cash flows. The City really wished to know in these times how we were going to beat the regulator and increase the cash flows and, hence, the share price. However, in the last two or three years, we and the City have recognised that the utility has a series of assets. These are both physical at the generation, and become more intangible at the customer level. The question now is how we can use these tangible and intangible assets to create new uses and, hence, new value for the enterprise.*

Transport company case

The following case reveals the effects of a poor track record on financing:

> *In the period 1995 to 2000, the intangibles information has been very poor in this company. For example, there have been many unexpected management changes. You know about these; our US Executive had a problem and our Chairman faced difficulties with his political activities. We really needed a good acquisition with good financial performance prospects to show added value. In the last quarter of 1999, we made a big acquisition in the US. We asked the fund managers for equity financing to pay for the US acquisition. Before the issue and before the management problems the share price was about XXX pence. Some of the major management events occurred during the equity issue and our share price dropped to 40%. Our capital raising was very much affected*

by this price change and we struggled to get the equity issue sold. We are still hoping to counteract these problems with our management and other intangibles in the share price. So, we hope that the US acquisition will help us in this respect.

This combination of fund manager and analyst processes were perceived as forming an informed context for fund managers and analysts to interpret new events and information. In particular, they were the outcomes of fund managers' and analysts' processing of *ex-ante* value-relevant company information. This adapted information played a central role in fund manager and analyst valuations of companies and in their subsequent decisions. As a result, they represented key means of intermediating company-supplied information into stock prices and asset returns.

Y4: Barriers to fund manager and analyst learning

Many barriers (Y4) existed to an effective disclosure interaction process. For example, the case companies observed considerable differences amongst fund managers in the performance of their common portfolio tasks. This was due to a variation in factors such as investment policies (stable *versus* volatile, passive *versus* active), time horizons, fund size, the scale of actual and potential ownership stakes, fund manager internal research capability and the degree of reliance on external research. Analysts exhibited a similar variation between buy-side and sell-side research styles, time horizons, independence and many other factors. As a result, there was some variation in aims, skills and competencies within the market for information across the regular contact group of core fund managers and key analysts. A major problem shared by the case companies, fund managers and analysts was the absence of a clear conceptual framework to understand and measure the role of intangibles in corporate value creation. The story and benchmarks were used as an interim solution to this problem. In addition, problems of bias, conflicts of interest, and errors were perceived amongst sections of the analyst and fund manager community. All of the above were seen as having the potential to adversely effect fund managers' and analysts' ability to process company-supplied information and, thus, generate an effective understanding and the confidence required to underpin the quality of their decisions as shown in these cases:

Technology company case

> *... in the e-commerce area, fund managers were very ignorant and were asking companies what was going to happen. One of the problems that the fund managers have is they have very little contact with the real business world except through the top management. This can be seen as a barrier to understanding companies and their intangibles and their contribution to value. Fund managers' decisions are not based on a full understanding of the company. They know terms like 'just in time' and they know this is the right thing to do but they do not really understand the concept even when they are taken round a factory and see the idea put into action. The kind of questions they ask under these circumstances often reveal the innocence of the fund managers.*

Insurance company case

> *You can divide up the analysts into the two extreme ends of the spectrum. One, in which we have the numbers-driven brokers' analysts who focus on the incremental changes in the numbers and not really on the ideas. We have difficulty with these analysts in getting over the nature of traditional intangibles and the newer kind of intangibles. At the other end of the spectrum you have the more qualitative analysts and fund managers who are more strategic thinkers. These really need some kind of discussion of the nature of our traditional business and the new kind of intangibles and they want much more in-depth information of what is going*

on here. At the strategic end, they want to hear more about the brands, the marketing strategy, and they also want to know how we are going to beat the opposition in the world of the future. They want to know how we are going to get the edge on the Internet providers and other competition. They are especially interested in the quality of management at all levels, so they want to look at top management and middle management. At present we are producing voluminous reports with every change in the industry and we are producing voluminous data; if you just look at our interim results you will see some of the data. The fund managers and analysts cannot really handle this massive detail and it needs to be boiled down to some essentials. Some kind of conceptual framework is required to put all of this together. If we had this we could communicate much more clearly what we are about and how we are adapting to the new circumstances in insurance.

Oil company case

What are the fund manager barriers to understanding the intangibles in this business? ... Number one, time: They don't have much time to see us as there are many company results coming out over the year and they may have up to two hundred and fifty companies in their portfolio and they must allocate time accordingly. Number two, they have a need to simplify; they must do this given the range of companies they are dealing with. Three, fashion such as this current focus on top management personality. Four, the nature of their capital allocation task. They are only allocating a certain amount of capital to countries and then to sectors and we are competing with XXX for them to own our shares and, therefore, this is a factor. Five, their portfolio view, they have to look at the whole portfolio as well as a specific company view.

These problems, or barriers, within analyst and fund manager decision processes were discussed fully in Holland and Johanson (2003).

The barriers manifested themselves as knowledge, uncertainty, ownership and management problems and revealed how company-side factors (high invisibles, poor news flow) interacted with fund manager-side or analyst-side factors (cognitive limitations, time pressure, lack of a conceptual framework, bias) to exacerbate these barriers.

The knowledge problem dealt with cases where these capital market actors failed to understand the importance of certain corporate intangibles. For example, in the case of human capital investment, they lacked the necessary understanding of the potential of human capital investment in a specific firm. The companies perceived that fund managers and analysts were very aware of top management human capital, but appeared to be poorly informed about other employee human capital and their role in value creation. The uncertainty problem concerned situations where even if capital market actors did understand the connection between human capital indicators and the strategic vision of the firm, they were probably hesitant about human capital investments, such as different management teams in a takeover, because they did not know if they could rely on these indicators. Questions of reliability and validity were evident with the scale of unknowns or invisibles in the corporate value-creation chain. These issues led fund managers and analysts to use easily observable proxies and methods to infer the existence of the invisibles in the value-creation process. This hesitation was probably connected to the lack of ownership of intangibles related to people; for example, because a company or fund manager could only rent competence and not own individual competence, the risk of losing this competence might be overly exaggerated. This danger was most evident in companies and sectors where there was a perceived shortage of top managerial talent, such as in the retail sector.

The management problem related to the fact that capital market actors were ultimately hesitant and indecisive, and that these problems arose because they did not know if any measures actually mattered in firms' management control processes. For example, did company management take necessary action when given adverse information on company intangibles such as poor customer satisfaction? Did fund managers take action on company-supplied data on intangibles, such as problems in management or board succession caused by a limited managerial labour market? In the case of fund managers, the likelihood of any action being taken was based on whether or not they saw clear links between the data on intangibles and the share price, as well as the extent to which they had confidence in this linkage. The problems of the fragility of this understanding have the potential to impede action. The problems of knowledge and uncertainty and of ownership and of management can be interpreted as outcomes or consequences of 'bounded rationality' (Simon, 1969).

These four problems of knowledge, uncertainty, ownership and management, were identified as being common within the fund manager and analyst value-creation chains, and created barriers to processing company-supplied information. In addition, cultural pressures within analyst and fund manager communities were viewed as contributors to these information barriers (Holland and Johanson, 2003). Such problems were exacerbated by additional market-induced problems of severe time constraints and conflicts of interest. Fund managers and analysts deliberately selected parts of the corporate information set that were considered value relevant at a point in time (Holland, 2004). The time pressures, changing market fashions and fads, periodic reporting cycles and preferences for a transient, price-sensitive information set, all revealed that market-side pressures narrowed down fund managers' and analysts' views about relevant information concerning intangibles. These pressures further contributed to the knowledge, uncertainty, ownership and management problems when processing company-supplied information.

Y5: Consensus in the market for information and new information

The case companies were aware that fund manager and analyst consensus was critical to the market and corporate disclosure contributed to a wider consensus about a company. This was apparent at an individual company level and was affected by sentiment about the sector, which in turn was influenced by the state of the broad economy. Such aggregation from individuals to a core consensus to a market consensus was based on: *(i)* corporate private disclosures; *(ii)* public disclosures; *(iii)* transaction exchanges amongst all parties; and *(iv)* an observation of market actions.

Corporate efforts to influence views were focused on the first two of the above levels. Influence of this nature was considered feasible, but it became less so at higher levels of aggregation, *ie.* those involving all fund managers and analysts at a sector and market level. As a result, the case companies were particularly interested in the nature and degree of this consensus amongst the core fund manager and analyst group. The fund managers consisted of, for example, the largest 20 to 30 individual core fund managers with overall ownership control, while the analysts consisted of individuals ranked by the company and others, as being in the top 10 to 15 in terms of influence and knowledge. This group of fund managers and analysts was thought to be the main influence on the wider information market and stock market and, hence, their private views could act as a rough proxy for wider market expectations and consensus. For example, they were thought to be the primary contributors to market-wide earnings and price expectations for the company and sector and these were manifest as consensus earning numbers.

The consensus was formed about qualitative factors such as the current corporate value-creation story, management succession, and likely strategic changes. They also concerned a consensus about the nature of the shared value-creation story to be found in a sector.

Oil company case

> *Meetings and other interactions between the company and the fund managers and the market extend over many years. You can think of a process consisting of many exchanges over time. The company begins by having information on how its intangibles create value. It discloses information on brands, management quality and technology, whatever it is. These qualitative factors are listed or ranked, in public or in the private world of opinion surveys and analysts. Fund managers get some idea of the net advantage that the company has relative to its competitors and amongst its peers and how this advantage arises from intangibles. Then in the private one-on-one meetings, this ranking and benchmarking becomes an important basis for private dialogue and for the promises made between the two parties. The fund managers build up their understanding of how these intangibles contribute to value, over a period of time. In the meetings companies are repeatedly making promises to deliver good performance. They are promising to deliver good strategy, high quality technology and effective brands and good quality disclosure systems and they are promising that these will lead to concrete financial performance. Over the next year, or few years, the company has to deliver these concrete performance targets and qualitative promises. It discusses in subsequent meetings whether it delivered the promises and how this was done. Taking this process in the round you can see that all of these interactions over time form a package of expectations and promises and measures about the future. It is in this package, between the company and its fund managers and the market at large, that we see that there is probably a price premium for brands, for technology, effectiveness, and quality of management.*

The consensus was also concerned with wider market views on the ranges of likelihood of corporate success with key intangibles. These involved a range of conventional numbers such as future earnings and price estimates. The range of corporate earning forecast numbers were amenable to statistical analysis, such as the calculation of means, medians and standard deviations, and these summary statistics were available from commercial services. The confidence in strategy and value-creation existed in the form of the degree of perceived convergence, consistency, and a common coherence of ideas and opinion amongst the core analysts and fund managers, as well as their degree of agreement on the chances of success. The variation around this central tendency was manifest in the unique interpretations or critiques of the corporate value-creation stories coming from a small number of analysts with strong reputations; this reflected many of the fund manager and analyst information processing barriers. The consensus and variation about earnings and other accounting and finance numbers was perceived as being interpreted within the value-creation story consensus and variation; this led, in turn, to market consensus, variation, and expectations about price.

The cases indicated that a high perceived consensus of qualitative factors such as the current corporate value-creation story formed a positive context for the consensus and variation about earnings and other accounting and finance numbers and increased the expected values and reduced the variance around these consensus forecast earnings.

Pharmaceuticals company case

> *There is an issue of confidence around these estimates of earnings and cash flows produced by analysts and used by the fund managers in their valuation. We talk to our major brokers' analysts and fund managers a lot. We also make fifty new releases or announcements a year. This is unusual for a company but it is just because of the size of our business portfolio and the range of drugs we are into. It is also because of the newsworthy nature of companies in this industry. As a result, we have a very active Investor Relations programme. The consensus forecast for earnings in this industry*

only function around a very narrow range because if you know our patents and our market share, our earnings are fairly predictable up to two or three years out. Of course, what goes on beyond that period is very uncertain and depends upon these intangibles and the growth prospects they produce for this enterprise. If there is a sudden, unexpected failure of a drug programme or a patent goes out of its time in an unexpected way then this will have an effect on the expected value and it also may increase the variance of these cash flows and, therefore, may make our share price more volatile. However, as I say, we are fortunate in the sense that we have this channel of communication through to a group of highly informed fund managers who are highly specialised in this industry and, therefore, it means there is an informed sector of the market that knows a lot about this very, very complex business. If you add to that the certainty of our cash flows over the short to medium term then this helps our stock price to be less volatile than one would expect from such a complex options-based and intangibles-based business.

Chapter six describes how the case companies observed a two-way learning process by analysts and fund managers concerning the links between earnings consensus estimates and the market consensus on value-creation stories and other qualitative information. This process created additional information for core fund managers and influential analysts.

The different kinds of consensus offered new ways for company managers to manage expectations; for example, they could increase the level of detailed disclosure about both the story and the earnings numbers, or they could vary the level of disclosure for qualitative *versus* quantitative information. They could also vary the degree of opportunism or bias for both forms of disclosure or vary this behaviour with each form.

For example, different levels of guidance could be given to the earnings consensus compared to the value-creation story consensus. The company could seek to down-play market expectations about earnings, so that investors did not expect too much and were, thus, less easily surprised by an unexpected adverse change on concrete numbers; such a change would obviously be higher if the firm had been too optimistic on earnings. The firm could also expend additional resources to ensure that the consensus around their value-creation stories, and other qualitative disclosures, was based on greater in-depth information, thereby creating a more informed climate around the story of the firm's future. Extensive narrative about competitive advantages and measures of key performance indicators could be used to support this more informed view. The differences suggest that consensus analysts earnings forecasts were likely to be less ambitious, but their detailed reports and strategy consensus might be more informed for the company. If adverse unexpected changes occurred in actual or forecast numbers, the companies felt they had 'discussion and understanding space' with the analysts to explain how they were going to solve the problem. If positive unexpected changes occurred in actual or forecast numbers the companies felt they had space to build on this. The qualitative story thus acted as an extra informed 'cushion' against surprises with the numbers. Chapter six, in particular the section on 'learning about analyst behaviour', provides more details about the way in which companies sought to manage analysts' and fund managers' consensus expectations.

Increased optimism could also be built into the story and into the 'correction' of the numbers, or a company could decide to be more optimistic and less easily checked, qualitative earnings forecast corrections. However, such opportunism and bias would eventually be understood by the market and be built into its pricing of company performance and disclosure behaviour. Indeed, whatever consistent mixture of detailed *versus* limited qualitative or quantitative disclosure, or of optimistic and biased behaviour, was adopted, this would eventually be discounted by the market and become the company 'market rating' for disclosure. The case companies were aware of this and generally sought such market ratings so as to reduce their equity cost of capital subject to the other choice issues described in chapter three.

Y6A: New company circumstances

The market consensus was fragile and could be easily disturbed by new corporate or market circumstances. In the cases, new company circumstances related to three major types of situations:

- When unexpected changes at the company level occurred. These normally involved: *(i)* surprise company events or unexpected performance; *(ii)* information about a fundamental change in the value-creation story; *(iii)* news relating to a key intangible; or *(iv)* confirmation of the risk relating to a company story.
- Where there were connected signals or surprises. These had an amplified effect and a much greater impact on the fragility of the market consensus and on price.
- When unexpected changes occurred outside the normal business domain, but revealed insights or surprises about the business domain.

The following two cases reveal a sudden change at company level and illustrate how this undermined the previous market consensus:

Insurance company case

> *Now ... the brokers' analysts are increasing their demands for information from us ... It has occurred because we have just had a new chief executive and finance director. In fact we have just had two finance directors, one only lasted four months. This has led the City to wonder whether he discovered some embarrassing*

secrets or, alternatively, he wasn't up to the job, or whether he had a big row with the new chief executive. Of course, they are looking carefully at the new finance director. I have told the new finance director to go out and have lunch with the top ten brokers' analysts and have a beer and a long chat with them and be fairly open with them and tell them "I'm new to the business and know a lot about finance but I am picking up the insurance business". He should, therefore, come clean and build trust and create a warm relationship with them.

Consumer goods company case

Recently, we faced major dislocation as we put two companies together. We particularly faced new problems in the market execution area in the first half-year as we joined together two teams and we have lost some market share. These problems were because the XXXX salesmen had different ideas to the YYYY salesmen. Now we have to spend a lot of time training the salesmen to ensure that they have a common approach to market execution. We think the improvements here will lead to increased market share. We found that the fund managers didn't really understand this … they think it is really about a quick firing of staff and then a focus on cost cutting. They don't really understand that it is about value creation.

Technology company case

The following case illustrates the high degree of fragility that developed in the presence of connected signals or surprises. If a combination of unexpected adverse changes such as: management problems; other real business developments; or a major shift of view by a key analyst occurred together, they could have much greater fragility and price effects compared to the sum of individual changes alone. Chapter six illustrates how the case companies developed 'responsiveness' to deal with this fragility.

> *Information about substantive areas of the business could be about new R&D expenditure, or that a new engine has passed an important safety test or certification test, or new information about a level of engine sales or it could be new information about the level of maintenance contracts. Good news about several of these occurring together can be quite a boost to price. If the news about a group of events goes the other way then we can get a bigger price drop than if these events had happened at different times. At present, we are vulnerable. Confidence factors surrounding the substantive information are very fragile here at present. The question is, why? Well, it could be that the company has a negative track record in terms of its financial performance. We have a reputation for destroying shareholders' wealth. One factor, our track record, is affecting the confidence factor. So, whatever the company says about its prospects the market discounts this. Any bad news about engine sales coinciding with a drop in R&D expenditure will have a big, big impact. The other day we announced an unexpected set of retirals of the old engines. This meant that the spares business and the maintenance business here was not going to be as large as possible and, hence, the cash flows arising from this were going to be smaller and riskier. We calculated that the drop in value was about £50m. However, the market price dropped by £750m. The question is, why? Well, the answer is that this was a signal about the kind of uncertainty that could occur with existing sales and future sales and future maintenance contracts.*

The fragility problem also arose due to internal company-side factors. These included a high exposure to uncertainty in real businesses as companies changed their economic processes from highly tangible assets and processes to new knowledge-intensive assets and less visible processes. If top management qualities, or other observable features were used as a proxy for the value-creation story, because of complexity or invisibility, then factors such as unexpected top management problems could magnify the effects and lead to major price drops and increase price volatility. This issue reflected a more general problem that arose if a proxy or a sub-set of company value-creation information was used as a sole source. In other companies, fragile earnings estimates and valuations occurred because of a failure to deliver on promises, or the existence of opportunistic pay schemes, or other factors that were deemed inappropriate by fund managers and as a result of excessive financial communication exposures, whereby the company was always the focus of the financial and public interest, such as in retail businesses, banks, national 'champions' or 'bellweathers'. This in turn created a more variable cost of equity capital.

Y6B: Market conditions

New market conditions included many different market sentiment effects at company and sector levels and these could also affect market consensus. Thus the 'dot-com' period of 1997-2000 had a negative effect on all the 'old economy' case companies; the subsequent switches of market fashion back to a focus on fundamentals altered the case companies' perceptions of the fragility of company understanding amongst fund managers and analysts.

Technology company case

> *... it is somewhat surprising to compare the way that we are treated when one looks at the new dot.com companies. We have released the full set of information about substantive issues in this business. These new dot.com businesses often do not have substantive businesses that make concrete products and there is*

very little information about them. Also, the confidence factor must be fairly new and not be based upon track record. The amazing thing is that these companies' prices seem to soar away. This shows the difference really between the well-known and the well-understood company, in terms of its production system and in terms of its financial performance and track record. This fashion has had an impact on us and we have had to figure how to adapt our technology story to this new internet world.

Consumer goods company case

... it's only seven months since the dot.com stocks started to crash. We do not have a high tech element in our business. The stock market seems to be valuing our brand in the existing business and our brand management and marketing skills are being applied here. However, this appears to be a major under-valuation; it seems the stock market has yet to come around and correctly value the growth in this business arising from the same brands, brand management, and markets being applied to new situations such as new overseas markets, or stretching the brands, or acquiring brands and improving them. We know we will come back into fashion, but the question is, when?

These new market conditions could also include sector-specific sentiment effects on companies. For example, both the insurance sector and the banking sector were considered to be out of market favour during 2000. This situation could change quickly, however, if macro forecasts began to alter.

Insurance company case

There are also many market confidence issues here. The general insurance industry and the non-life insurance industry lost its reputation with the market. This is because of cavalier management which misused excess capital and if we sold a business now for £500 million the market would be desperate for us to hand it back to the fund managers. The question the fund managers and analysts are asking now is: is this new kind of management in insurance any different or any better? So, really, we have a negative intangible here. It will only be dealt with when our story is believed. Our story about value-creation through these intangibles will only be believed when we produce concrete results.

At the company level, market issues included, a narrow focus on a current 'running' story relevant to a company, a very short 'attention cycle' or 'news cycle' concerning a company or sector, changing market and sector sentiment leading to changing valuation views and information needs, and sudden stock price, company and market, changes independent of company disclosure or actions. These market pressures could lead to the analysts and fund managers by-passing company fundamentals, and focusing instead on single company actions as the sole basis for valuation.

Holland (2004) describes the more general change process in the capital markets and its impact on company disclosure content. The increasing sophistication, globalisation and concentration of financial markets - and of the market for information - were changing analyst and fund manager information demands upon companies. Unanticipated changes in market fashion, sentiment, and growing shareholder pressures in these markets were having similar effects. The case companies noted that these developments had altered the contingent nature of the information demands made upon them. The market change worsened the problems that the analysts and fund managers faced in processing intangibles information within their valuation models and other portfolio-level and sector-level decisions and, hence, exacerbated the fragility of consensus information.

Feedback

The case companies probed the individual fund managers and analysts during their interactions for feedback. Despite this probing and feedback, the markets' adaptation of their company-supplied information was only partially understood by the case companies.

The flow of the company value-creation information components into the stock price were impeded by various barriers (Y4) in the fund manager and analyst evidence-seeking process. The corporate value-creation information was adapted by fund managers and analysts, and by changing company and market circumstances, as it flowed into the price and other market parameters. This adaptation was only partly understood by the case companies.

Retailer case

The following case reveals how company information was intermediated into stock prices by fund managers and analysts.

> *An interesting question is how intangibles, like management qualities get into the stock price? Well, we think it happens over time as some kind of cumulative learning about what each major intangible element is and its track record in contribution to value. We can look at our experience here. We have a track record over time in terms of innovation and in terms of competing effectively. Now these kind of track record intangibles get into the stock price and there is a premium to reflect our capabilities in this respect. If we put out a forecast then the fund managers and the analysts value our forecast higher than our competitors XXXX or YYYY. This is because of our track record. They place more reliance on us delivering that forecast. In other words, we have built up their confidence and the market has learnt this over time. Track record is an intangible, or soft information and this gets into our stock*

price ... They are not based upon formal measures but are based on the learning by fund managers and analysts over time. This learning might be about an individual and can be transferred. So, if you just look at management quality, as an example, if you think of our competitor XXXX and their frequent changes of management over the past two or three years, they have had two stock price collapses and we think they are related to changes in the perception of management quality. Of course, their new chief executive has just come in and he is a top-class manager. He is now given the benefit of the doubt because of his previous track record and the stock price at XXXX has reflected that in the last couple of days. The problem is that he now has to deliver. So you can see that it is not clear how it gets into the price, but it certainly is a contributor to it.

The case companies developed some qualitative insights into the market consensus from a careful reading of the top 20 or so analysts reports or through a dialogue with the top fund managers, analysts and traders just after earnings announcements. These market participants commented directly on the company value-creation story and benchmark measures, and also fed back information to companies by their observable market actions. Companies such as MORI conduct benchmarking surveys of fund managers and analysts for a firm's sector and this provided the companies with some insights about the consensus; this in turn helped isolate the lists of key company, or sector, value-creation factors which affected fund managers' and analysts' opinions as well as the share price. Factors such as management quality were ranked and benchmarked relative to a company track record or target, a key competitor or across a whole sector. In some cases these factors were broken down into constituent elements and these were ranked according to their perceived importance. It was critical for companies to 'be on the lists' and, hopefully, to be in the top quartile. These sources provided the case companies with some understanding of what information was contained in the market consensus and hence what corporate-supplied information was likely to be in the stock price.

Consensus and specific earnings estimates and other statistics were also available from commercial services. All of these sources could potentially be used to summarise a 'market story' of company value creation and to assess the general confidence in this story as well as estimated earnings and price. However, the case companies knew they were guessing what information fund managers, analysts, and traders were using in their decisions.

Information on the changing consensus in the market for information was also available as market feedback in the form of observed changes in collective, or 'herd', behaviour such as trading, investing and share-holding, of the major fund managers, as well as alterations in behaviour and expectations of outlier fund managers and analysts. The changes in the observed collective behaviour of major fund managers, such as increased stakes in high technology stocks, provided information regarding the inferred consensus of these major market players. A shift in outlier fund manager behaviour, for example, out of equities and into cash, provided information on their unique expectations about companies. Commercial services were employed to find out about changing ownership structures and to deduce and infer which fund managers were involved in, often concealed, equity transactions. These observed actions and inferred expectations were often backed up by public statements by 'herd' (consensus) and outlier fund managers as well as by the views expressed in private one-to-one meetings. Similar changes in action, behaviour and expectation could be observed in the collective and outlier behaviour of the major sell-side analysts.

As a result, the case companies closely observed the impact of private interactions and corporate voluntary disclosure on publicly observable price, volatility, liquidity and cost of capital market outcomes.

The simultaneous disclosure of corporate information and the observation of the stock market response created major learning opportunities for the case companies; fund managers and analysts further amplified stock market price and volatility responses, to company disclosure, and other sources, back to companies *via* their direct comments on these market changes.

The case companies were able to infer the nature of non-observable stock market outcomes, such as the quality of the market information set, from an active dialogue with traders and other market participants. More specifically, the companies directly asked traders, fund managers and analysts how they valued the company, and what they thought was in the company price; they tried to relate this data to company-supplied information. In addition, the firms attempted to identify gaps and misunderstandings amongst their core fund managers and analysts, and hence deduce: *(i)* what information was contributing to the range of price expectations; and *(ii)* what information was not in the price.

It was difficult at times to get 'evidence' about the information in the share price, especially when it was of a soft, impressionistic nature. However, when some precise, specific events arose, or a relative change in benchmark position occurred, the case companies were able to connect these to observable price movements. Such learning meant that the firms developed their own ideas of what kinds of information was likely to be price-sensitive over time (see also Holland and Stoner, 1996) and they were also aware of the UKLA's list of price-sensitive information categories.

As a result, there was a considerable amount of corporate learning regarding these interactions and market outcomes; these represented important means of exploring the way in which the value-creation story and benchmarks got into the price and, hence, what corporate supplied information was in the stock price. However, the case companies knew that they were guessing about what fund managers, analysts and traders were surmising about the information contained in the share price. The above observations, probing, dialogue and feedback created corporate perceptions about the types of corporate supplied information that were contained in the price.

Table 2 summarises the dominant categories of corporate supplied information on intangibles perceived by the case companies to be in the stock price.

Table 2 - Information perceived to be in the stock price

Historic and future-oriented intangibles information concerning:

- Quality of top management, and a shared vision with middle management;
- Confidence and trust in top management and board unity;
- Clarity of, and promises about, strategy;
- Innovative capability, brand management skills, R&D effectiveness and other key intangibles in a company's competitive advantage, including connections between them and promises about them;
- Consistency of delivery, strategic and financial performance delivery and execution, execution risks and promises about performance;
- Scale of unknowns in the value-creation process, business uncertainty, the extent of strategic options and growth opportunities in the business;
- Clarity of financial communications, quality of fund manager and analyst relations.

Financial tangible numbers:

- Quality and forecastability of earnings and cash flows;
- Categories of key cash flows and recent changes;
- Price, power and margins in key areas of business and key financial ratios;
- Key tangible assets and liability valuations;
- Earnings and cash flows over relatively certain horizon periods (*eg.* 2 years).
- Earnings and cash flow generating or sustaining capability beyond this horizon.

The case companies differed in terms of their unique advantages of the factors listed in Table 2; they also varied in terms of the scale of the unknown in the value-creation process, business uncertainty and the degree of their strategic options. For example, those high on a list of these factors were perceived to have much 'softer' or fragile information in their stock price, while firms low on the list were perceived to have more credible information and more easily forecastable cash flows and earnings.

Each company, therefore, had some unique 'model' of what company-supplied information was used in its valuation and in its price; this perspective had a strong influence on their financial communications behaviour. The following two cases illustrate the case specific valuation model.

Media company

Value was a function of the tangible assets, TV licences, brands, relationships, management quality and management track record, employees, media talent as follows:

> *Our tangibles are bricks and mortar. The near-tangibles are things like the TV licences which, if they were to shoot up from £5 million to £10 million for the cost of renewal, then this would affect our share price. The next category we can move on to are the valuable intangibles such as top management qualities, track record, brands and relationships with other TV firms and advertisers and with our viewers and our readers. These particular categories are amongst our important intangibles; they directly affect value. The top management part of these involve our ability to facilitate deals and acquire new businesses. This increases our revenue and cash flows. It will increase the EBITDA before exceptional items and, of course, this will help us improve our share price. So, the valuable*

intangibles are pretty important. The final group, the intangible intangibles such as celebrity talent, are less valuable here.

Insurance company

Corporate value was a function of strategy, management quality, brand names, distribution channels, relations with Independent Financial Advisors, relations with consumers, innovation in products and distribution as follows:

> *Brands are thought to be very important in our business but to some extent you can see brands as being full of platitudes. We really need new brand research comparing our brands against other companies in the financial sector … We really need to have a much clearer idea of what the characteristics are of a brand and how they contribute to cash flows and to value. However, we have developed the SSSS brand in our Internet bank and this is successful. It really took off because it was backed by the parent company brand. We have been quite innovative in using technology to develop new distribution channels and adapting ones. We are also selling a wider range of insurance products down each one of these channels in a more sophisticated way. These are the means by which the company gets the sales which produces the cash flows, which produces value. These are the means to drop the cost of acquiring each unit of business and, hence, make sure the residual cash flows, or the margins, are very much higher and, hence, increase the share price. These are the critical ingredients in our share price.*

Cost of capital

The case companies assumed that the stock market would build in, or discount, corporate disclosure behaviour; this was in turn expected to impact on the cost of equity capital. Stable, high quality disclosure, and informed market information concerning the company, were expected to be discounted in the price and lead to a reduction in the cost of capital.

This cost of capital 'information premium' was expected to remain stable relative to competitors with lower quality disclosure. The market was thought to learn over time how to price company disclosure and its cumulative impact on information markets; it therefore included an expectation about future disclosure and its market impact.

Unexpected deviations from this expectation were believed to impact upon share prices. For example, a negative surprise in disclosure was expected to lead to a sudden drop in the stock price and an increase in the cost of capital. The case companies, therefore, had strong market-based incentives to maintain high disclosure standards and to avoid surprises.

A similar cost of equity-capital premium was also associated with top management and board qualities as well as with the effectiveness of the wider hierarchical value-creation process. This effect was built into market prices as the market developed an expectation about the future quality of management and the hierarchical value-creation process. The case companies, therefore, had similar strong market incentives to maintain high management and board standards and to avoid succession and resignation surprises.

Both the 'information premium' and the 'top management premium' were expected to lower the cost of capital and produce value increments to factors V1 to V5; these were captured in factors V6 and V7 and in the APV equation in chapter four.

Summary

This chapter has described additional elements to the model of financial communication. These included a disclosure interaction between the case companies and the markets, the shareholder wealth maximising 'atmosphere' of these private interactions, the barriers, feedback and perceived outcomes arising in these markets and the fragility of these outcomes. These have provided many practical insights for companies developing their financial communications policy. This chapter has provided a practical frame of reference to analyse how companies continuously interact with, and influence, fund managers, analysts and the stock market through regular disclosure of *ex-ante* value-relevant information. The chapter has also made clear that the case companies expended considerable resources on influencing the evidence-checking processes of fund managers and analysts, to minimise the effects of any barriers, to probe both the information understood by these parties and the information in the stock price. The fragility of these factors and the growing shareholder wealth pressures from private meetings, and market feedback, make it clear that such actions must have clear shareholder wealth management aims.

Chapter Six

Corporate Learning and Improvements in Financial Communication

Chapter six explores the ways in which cumulative, multi-period, corporate learning and perceptions about the market outcomes of disclosure, reinforced by fund managers during subsequent one-to-one meetings, fed back into corporate disclosure. This feedback determined corporate disclosure based on learnt preferences and could be broken down into: disclosure content; disclosure choice; disclosure behaviour; disclosure structures; and disclosure processes.

Disclosure content

Chapter five described how the case companies: linked fragments of information on intangibles; created a wider picture of the future; and made promises about the value-creation process.

In addition, the growing shareholder wealth management pressure in private meetings and in public discourse led the UK case companies to understand that their corporate disclosure by top management had to have a clear shareholder wealth management aim. Ezzamel *et al.* (2002) revealed how intense these shareholder wealth pressures were in a US context, demonstrating the way in which a CEO interpreted these stock market demands and transmitted these pressures internally through corporate strategy. In general terms, the growing shareholder wealth management pressure meant that the UK case companies learnt that corporate disclosure:

- Had to be narrow, focused, and bounded, and have a clear shareholder wealth management aim and be provided mainly by top management.
- Would increasingly be driven by a permanent and steady demand from the market for shareholder wealth management information.
- Take place in the context of a constant shareholder wealth management aim, but that the value-relevant information required to demonstrate this would constantly change.

The disclosure content was influenced, in part, by the ever-present financial reporting cycle and by the information standards set by such formal reporting mechanisms. However, this cycle had a more fundamental effect. Holland (1998) reported that companies were aware that they would have to explain their strategy to their core fund managers some time shortly after earnings announcements were made. Companies thought ahead to their fund manager meetings and timed their internal planning cycle so that they could have their most up-to-date strategic review ready for the external institutional communications cycle following an earnings announcement. As a result, each case company had an extensive internal debate to identify and clarify strategy and decide upon the main message to be communicated. The existence of external fund manager monitoring sharpened up this process because senior executives knew that they would have to communicate effectively during fund manager meetings and presentations. External advisers played a central role in this internal debate and helped the case companies to clarify their primary strategic messages and to script all senior executives in their understanding of this strategy. The intention was that they should 'all sing from the same hymn sheet' during these meetings.

The following two cases shows how companies decided what kind of information should be released to the market:

Insurance company case

Really, a key job of investor relations and the finance director in this business is to make the story links clear and to tell the story as coherently as possible and also, when these concrete connections are made, when they occur, to make it absolutely clear in the market that this has happened. In other words, we have to show how the quality of management and its effectiveness has had an impact upon tangibles in the business. We have to ensure that the analysts and the fund managers meet our management and can assess things like the quality of management, their effectiveness and the coherence of strategy.

Oil company case

We are aware of fund managers' needs and we try and think in the appropriate way. We, therefore, try to think into their mindset and we try and demonstrate through the above approach in terms of the quality of our communications. There are four key elements in which we compete on in terms of our ability to communicate to the City. We try to ensure that we get across the key management intangibles. They are: (1) the quality of management; (2) the clarity of strategy; (3) our track record or, if you like, our ability to execute and deliver promises; and (4) our ability to lay out our plans for the future at the level of group and at key business unit levels and demonstrate progress against these plans. These are really the four key elements we are trying to communicate on. We try and do this well and we compete on communicability and we see this is a key intangible.

Adaptiveness

The case companies also had developed experience of how to let a story evolve or adapt in response to: *(i)* changing corporate processes;

(ii) changing views of key fund manager and analysts; *(iii)* listener competence and the complexity of their valuation models; and *(iv)* changes in market sentiment. Despite this, the companies were wary of adapting their story too much to the conflicting needs and ideas existing amongst the core contact group of fund managers and analysts. More specifically, the case companies learnt that the prevailing market concept of value-relevant information, required to demonstrate the shareholder wealth management aim to fund managers, was transient and varied according to changes in market structure, fashion, and sophistication. At times, such as during the 'Dot.com' period of 1997-2000, the case companies argued that company-based value-creation information was not value relevant in any significant sense. They argued that fund managers and analysts only looked at stock market changes and the portfolio actions of other fund managers as their primary source of information. In periods before 1997 and after 2000, company value-creation or fundamental information was thought to be combined with market-derived information to form the value-relevant information set. The interactive learning with information market participants affected companies' views about what represented an appropriate value-creation process and associated value-relevant information. During the dot.com period the case companies, all drawn from the 'old' economy, developed internet strategies in response to the prevailing fashion.

Insurance company case

The following case shows how a company learnt to adapt its disclosure content to meet the varying needs of fund managers:

> *When we meet our institutional shareholders or group of twenty or thirty fund managers in one-on-ones then we will vary our communication policy to these fund managers. If these are new fund managers and they don't really know us then much of the meeting will be given to an overview and try to explain the nature of the business. However, if they are well known, if the*

> *fund managers know us as a company well, then the agenda is quite different. We start with last year's promises and arguments and explore these in greater depth and see if they have been delivered. We may discuss specific strategic moves discussed last time around and whether they have been implemented. We may discuss perceived weak parts of the business such as some of the fund management business sold off recently because it didn't fit in with the overall strategy. We will discuss where the growth areas are going to be and whether we will seek to grow the business in particular ways.*

The case companies had learnt about the limitations of fund managers and others, especially when major changes occurred in strategy. As a result they developed their message and 'signposting' to fund managers through complex public disclosures (see Chapter 4 for details).

The case companies also recognised that they needed to maintain a stable disclosure protocol, or set of established conventions, surrounding the disclosure of the information package; this consisted of a combination of: *(i)* coherent corporate story telling; *(ii)* a track record in keeping promises; *(iii)* reliable performance; and *(iv)* persistence in all of these elements. The companies recognised that they required a coherent story and needed to 'live with their story' through positive and negative events over time. Regular reinforcement of the story through consistent corporate action was also important; the firms needed to continuously disclose information about the story as both positive and negative events occurred. The case companies also knew that if they could demonstrate a track record in the value-creation story and in strategy execution that revealed consistency with the story and flexibility in successfully making changes, then their disclosure would gain credibility. However, as noted in chapter four, this financial communications aim could be constrained by the need for secrecy.

Chemical company case

The following case reveals how important persistence was in the story telling, execution and performance:

> *To rebuild our story to reflect the major changes in this business we must have a series of boring messages about strong strategy and evidence of it working in terms of good financial performance. We must do this each quarter and each half year and each year, year in, year out, over time. We must increasingly convince the market of our strategy in terms of the value creation along these speciality chemical chains and we must also show concrete output in terms of these stories. Once we start doing that then confidence will return. This is probably the main reason why the share price has dropped so much .... We spend a lot of time educating the analysts, especially the chemical analysts. We have still not got them to appreciate this view, that we are a high quality business. The question is, if we cannot persuade them of our new speciality chemicals nature then what is the chance of us doing it for the rest of the fund managers and analysts in the market? We really have to persist here in terms of explaining how we have changed the strategy and we need to keep repeating it but we need to demonstrate it, in terms of the cash flows being created. This will feed back and they will, eventually, believe the story about us being a knowledge-intensive industry and being able to differentiate our products and create high price margins and monopoly in some areas and, hence, high profits.*

Disclosure choices

Chapter four explored the ways in which the case companies sometimes needed to maintain some secrecy over their private disclosure, and to match disclosure benchmark norms and seek high rankings for their corporate disclosure quality.

Transport company case

The following case reveals how a case company learnt to make disclosure choices between financial reporting and private meetings:

> *Why not use the financial report for disclosure of information about intellectual capital and intangibles? Perhaps we might be able to do this if we did quarterly reporting and could also put the spotlight on certain key themes such as productivity or cost-cutting approaches or staff training or incentive schemes. We might be able to expose more information about intangibles through such a detailed theme approach. However, the basic weakness of the financial report is that it is a one-way view of the world from the company out to investors. It is often a rosy and positive view. It is, therefore, not very good at disclosing information about some of the more critical intangibles. You really need one-on-one meetings and the exchange of ideas to really get over these items of information. It is in the one-on-one meetings that the fund managers can ask questions. This is not really possible with the financial report. This is possibly the only way in which the fund manager can get information on human capital in the enterprise. They can talk to us as top managers and they can see us in action, but this is not really possible in any kind of financial report. Given that this is the critical intangible in most companies, then one-on-ones are going to stay with us and the financial report will never be able to handle this kind of information. It is clearly best if the fund managers can spend one hour on their questions. They can ask much better quality questions. This is better for us and for them and we both learn from this dynamic interchange. They can, therefore, assess our ability as well as listening to our answers and we learn more about the intangibles in the business as a result of this dynamic interchange with us.*

The above disclosure choice relates to Gibbins *et al.* (1990) concept of disclosure predisposition, which they define as a 'stable preference for the way disclosure is managed'. In the present study, this included stable disclosure policies and incorporated preferences for the use of stories plus benchmarks as primary disclosure means, as well as elements of ritualism, opportunism, and bias in such disclosure behaviour. In the case companies, predisposition also involved setting up responsive value-relevant information systems. This included the use of flexible, broad information categories in the value-creation process, regular private meetings and a stable disclosure protocol. Predisposition was also based on understanding the changing definition of value-relevant information and of deviations from the consensus. In addition, the story-telling and benchmarking of the effectiveness of specific intangibles, were critical to the disclosure of information about these specific intangibles.

Disclosure behaviour

Optimism and opportunism

The case companies learnt that three processes prevented them from freely exercising their bias towards optimism and opportunism during the one-to-one private meetings.

First, core fund managers 'look on the dark side' or focused on the downside risk and this forced the case companies to talk more about downside risks. The sell-side analysts were considered to be more interested in information about the upside and downside risks that could encourage buy or sell recommendations. Together, fund managers and analysts forced the case companies to talk more about the wider set of risks that they faced. The fund managers also saw the public disclosure of earnings and formal company presentations in private as a minimum level of disclosure; they expected private information to exceed this public and semi-public disclosure when they interrogated the case companies in private.

As a result, the case companies faced informed fund managers who concentrated on:

- the downside risk and probing the possibilities of major losses, as they sought to assess whether or not there was a 'floor' to a company's valuation.
- probing the quantitative and qualitative promises made previously in private, seeking to deepen and extend those promises; and
- observing and probing intangibles, such as management quality and coherence of strategy, competitor's strategy, management's understanding and ability to respond and carry out these activities.

This intense probing could only be done by well-researched, large fund managers with economies of scale in research and analysis. Small investors were not capable of demanding such access and of conducting such analyses, and they could not put the same pressure on management to disclose information about downside risks and move beyond public disclosure levels. Therefore, the market for information, especially its fund manager element, placed overt pressure on companies to counterbalance their desire to talk only about the 'bright-side of life'; this also revealed that a critical function of the one-to-one meetings was to counterbalance this corporate opportunism and bias.

Secondly, each case company faced external benchmarks for 'good' private disclosure. These were set competitively in the market as well as by company-specific private behaviour and promises. For example, the coherence of strategy, management quality, brand or R&D effectiveness and quality of board level governance were all benchmarked in a relative, sector-specific way. As a result of fund manager and analyst pressure, the companies also revealed details about their specific intangibles and changes in their relative benchmark measures; specific benchmark changes were placed in the context of the larger value-creation story and any changes in the wider story were clarified.

Thirdly, the accumulated learning over many periods created an awareness in companies of the penalties and incentives associated with opportunistic behaviour and helped control any opportunistic bias during private disclosure. However, the case companies only felt the pressure to adopt more balanced positive and negative disclosures when they were faced by probing and informed fund managers during private dialogues. The companies did not willingly release this information, nor did they formally not disclose it in their presentations, public disclosure documents or communication channels unless it involved a well-publicised problem, a profits warning, or they were faced by a clear regulatory requirement.

Consumer goods company case

The following case illustrates how one of the case companies learnt to modify its behaviour, building trust and understanding by setting clear targets, using a simple business model, and by keeping promises.

> *We tell the market what our targets are and report back to the market at the end of the year. So, we will talk about five per cent in terms of gross margins and so much in terms of overall growth of the business. We also expect that by the end of the year we will be able to talk about medium-term objectives over three to five-years rather than one-year objectives. So, you may say that the top line (sales) growth we aim for is about five per cent with a profit growth of ten per cent. We say our general targets are the four, eight, twelve targets; four per cent volume growth, eight per cent gross margin and twelve per cent profit growth. These targets are very important. They are a means to try to take the guessing out of the numbers. This is the job of the analysts trying to estimate our earnings for the next period. We are trying to simplify this by telling them what our targets are, and then they can focus their estimates round these targets. Of course, the targets are not what the numbers are going to be at the end of the day and they are not*

our estimates of what our future earnings are going to be. They are what they are, targets. By setting these targets it transforms investor relations. We are trying to show that we are people who deliver the promise. We hope that we will deliver and the market will believe us over time and, therefore, trust builds up. The benchmark company for us is XXXX. It is a very similar business to ourselves and they have had growth in forty successive quarters. They have the high trust of the market and this is what we would like to do. This is why we have been explicit on our targets. We also try to keep our business model very simple so that it can be understood by fund managers and analysts. We tell the market where we are going to put investment which is mainly in media marketing this year. We also explain how we are going to control working capital. The new parent company here is very good at this and we are trying to reduce our working capital to a negative value. We tell the market the business is self-funding for organic expansion. We think this kind of simple, clear-cut business model and clear targets are going to build up the trust of the market. So we are deliberately trying to build up this intangible, our reputation, for saying we are going to do something and then achieving it. It creates certainty and security and confidence in the company and in communications and investor relations and we are building up intangibles that affect the share price. We know that the market puts a very high premium on clarity, on certainty and on confidence and it hates uncertainty. Therefore, we need to get this right in our basic business, in our normal organic business without growth.

The same case company also altered its disclosure content once it had developed trust:

Once we have established this trust we can get over our growth prospects. So, once they have confidence in our steady business and they believe we deliver our promises we can talk about growth prospects. We think they will believe us, and this expected growth will go into the share price. So, we will get a correct rating for our business and this is what we are after. UK companies are not very good at making explicit their targets for the future. They can't tell you their estimates of cash flows. There is no problem with them making targets, this is perfectly legitimate, but of course they cannot make estimates. US and French companies are much better at making explicit their targets.

Surprises and deviations

The case companies expended considerable effort on the strategic value-creation story consensus, because insiders, such as the core fund managers and leading analysts, expected to be the 'least surprised' group in the market place.

Telecommunications company case

Our Investor Relations Director was an accountant; that means he can talk credibly with brokers' analysts about their models and the content of their models. He can, therefore, give comfort and credibility to these models. The analysts didn't really get this before with the previous Investor Relations Director. Providing this kind of comfort and credibility is the heart of financial communication. This ensures that the brokers' analysts' models are realistic. By this we are trying to be prudent with them, but are not too downbeat in terms of the realism in the models. We also prefer to surprise them on the upside not on the downside. Some people may take the view that the investor relations job is to create a rose-tinted view of the world and we are the spin-doctor.

Companies did not, of course, expect to be surprised by their own announcements. However, they could be very surprised by the market reaction to their results or other corporate actions. The companies expected core fund managers to be the least-surprised group because they had ownership power over companies, access to an in-depth private dialogue, internal analyst support and access to the external analysts' reports, as well as public domain information. The companies expected highly ranked influential analysts to be the next least-surprised group because they had research expertise and reputation power over companies, operated as sector specialists, had some access to a private dialogue and had considerable public domain information.

Finally, non-core fund managers and analysts and small uninformed investors were expected to be more surprised. Differences were therefore expected in the surprise factor across the core segments of the market for information.

The core fund managers and analysts were expected to fully understand the main value implications of the corporate value-creation story and be able to interpret the impact of changing events on the story in a more sophisticated and accurate way than could uninformed investors. Earnings announcements and observed corporate actions were thought to contain a lower surprise or unanticipated element for these core fund managers and analysts than the wider market; if this least-surprise state did not occur then they were in a position to take adverse action against the company.

These issues of consensus, and least surprise were becoming more and more important to the case companies as the invisible and intangible elements of corporate value creation increased. The case companies and core fund managers and analysts were exchanging much more information in private about the role of intangibles in value creation. The companies ensured that the story was widely understood by their core fund managers and analysts and was designed to reduce the potential for surprise about forecast numbers such as earnings. An attempt was made to jointly reduce ignorance about both the qualitative value-creation factors and the expected output numbers; as a result, earnings and story surprises were jointly minimised.

Deviations from a consensus on historic promises or from expectations

Two kinds of deviation from the consensus mattered to the case companies. The first concerned a difference between the current market consensus and the current company view. The second concerned differences between the historic consensus and what actually happened.

For example, in the first instance, if major information asymmetry was perceived between the current market earnings consensus, relative to the company view, then the case companies had to announce this publicly as price-sensitive information. Considerable care had to be taken afterwards in privately discussing these numbers with fund managers and analysts to ensure that additional price-sensitive information was not released in private. Once this action was undertaken - and the new value-creation ideas and concepts were in the public domain - the companies could then use private one-to-one meetings and other private communication channels to freely discuss, in detail, the much less precise, much vaguer set of concepts surrounding the value-creation story, and hence ensure that the core fund managers and analysts fully understood the story. The following case provides insights into how consensus on value creation interacted with consensus on earnings.

Pharmaceutical company case

> *There is an issue of confidence around these estimates of earnings and cash flows produced by analysts and used by the fund managers in their valuation. As a result, we talk to brokers' analysts and fund managers a lot … . The consensus forecast for earnings in this industry only functions round a very narrow range because if you know our patents and our market share, our earnings are fairly predictable up to two or three years out. Of course, what goes on beyond that period is very uncertain and depends upon these intangibles and the growth prospects they produce for this*

enterprise. If there is a sudden, unexpected failure of a drug programme or a patent goes out of its time in an unexpected way then this will have an affect on the expected value and it also may increase the variance of these cash flows and, therefore, may make our share price more volatile.

In the second instance, when a large difference occurred between a historic market consensus and what actually happened, either for earnings or the value-creation story, then this was checked for consistency against the old or original story relating to these actual outcomes. If this was a negative deviation, *ie.* where the actual story or earnings were worse than expected, this created a negative track record and a negative effect on the credibility of the current story. If it was a positive deviation, *ie.* where the actual story and earnings turned out better than expected and promised, then this contributed to a positive track record and had a positive effect on the credibility of the current story. However, negative effects only had to occur over one or two periods to have an effect on credibility whereas, in contrast, positive effects had to accumulate over many periods to create company credibility. Thus, there was asymmetric learning and different responses by market participants to the different kind of track records and hence an asymmetric payoff for disclosure behaviour.

For example, case Company X - with good financial performance in 40 successive quarters - had high credibility and the confidence of its core fund managers; this was reflected in its share price which, in turn, reflected the fund managers' confidence about the value-creation story involving the creation of knowledge-intensive strategic options and their exercise, as well as the evidence of their ultimate success and successful strategic execution. A similar premium was built into the confidence and credibility (intangible) factors surrounding the value-creation story about these elements. If this company had an unexpected bad quarter result or another unexpected event such as chief executive departure, then the impact on its share price could be huge. Such an effect would arise because the confidence factors in the overall value-creation story were questioned and perhaps lost; new questions could also be asked about the option creation and exercise process.

In contrast, case Company Y, in the same industry and with a similar value-creation process - but with erratic quarterly results over the past 40 quarters - already had low credibility and there was low confidence in its value-creation story; this was reflected in a higher cost of equity capital and a discount or reduction in the price. However, if this company experienced an unforeseen quarterly result then this had less impact on its share price.

Both companies were subject to the vagaries of stock market sentiment relative to the sectors they were in. Company X expected to be less exposed than Company Y to external market shocks because its intangibles suggested that it had a greater responsiveness to whatever fashions or dramatic events were driving stock market sentiment. However, as demonstrated above, it also had a much greater exposure to an internal company shock arising from an unanticipated failure, or under-performance, somewhere along its value-creation process.

Analyst error and bias

The discussion above indicates that the case companies perceived the value of the interaction between: the informed fund managers' and analysts' concerning future value-creation stories; and earnings and other estimates. Historical observation of strategic events, as well as the reporting of earnings and other accounting and finance numbers (*eg.* dividends), were thought to be used by fund managers and analysts as 'reality checks' on the historic corporate value-creation stories. In addition, as outlined in the previous section, the sign of the variance between expectations and actual results affected the credibility of such stories in the forecast period. These observations allowed fund managers and analysts to understand how corporate value-creation generated both stable and volatile elements relevant to corporate income and other accounting and finance numbers, and these then provided the basis for estimates of future numbers and for revisions in value-creation stories. The case companies learnt that this process created additional information for core fund managers and influential analysts.

The case companies also learnt that the interaction between qualitative and quantitative disclosures varied depending on the forecasting horizon, for example: six months; six months to two years; and beyond two years.

In the short (three to six month) period ahead, the case companies considered earnings forecasts to be major drivers of valuation. Company disclosure of relatively stable value-creation stories provided the means to reduce surprises when changes occurred in earnings estimates. The firms also perceived these as being the means by which core fund managers could place in context or counteract any inaccuracy, bias or optimism built into analysts earnings forecasts and any subsequent revisions made to these. For example, forecast inaccuracy was likely to reduce in response to new information becoming available closer to the event. As the announcements period approached and accuracy improved, analysts were also likely to use their revisions to remove any exaggeration or reduce mistaken or over-optimistic estimates. The latter may have been produced for wider broker house reasons such as boosting security sales or issues.

The improvement in forecasting earnings as the horizon declined was thought to arise from: *(i)* a combination of new public information concerning observable events; and *(ii)* the case companies' use of a 'drip feed' of private qualitative information about progress in corporate value-creation processes to correct perceived analyst errors. The latter reveals how the earnings forecasting process was, in part, a joint construction between the company and its analysts, relating to their use of dialogue to close the information gap between them.

The highly informed core fund managers were thought to be in a stronger position, and could use their understanding of case company value-creation stories to recognise some analyst forecast inaccuracies; such biases could then be discounted, especially if the fund managers knew the track record of the sector specialist analyst relative to a company. They were also considered to be in a position to interpret such forecast revisions, particularly if the revisions were consistent with or differed from the expected company story outcomes.

Such problems of inaccuracy, bias or optimism built into short-term analysts' earnings forecasts, were thought to decline with company-side and market for information-side factors. Therefore, increased simplicity, and stability, of the corporate value-creation story, the clarity of its links with financial performance, high corporate credibility, lower opportunism and bias, and a stable joint track record of story and performance over time, were all likely to reduce these problems. The problems were also thought to decline with increased reputation of the analysts, *ie.* lower opportunism and bias, track record, time following the company and sector, and size of the broker house relative to the company.

In the forecast period of six months to two years, the case companies recognised that the analysts earnings forecast accuracy was likely to be poor and not much better than a prediction arising from a mechanistic use of the earnings time series. At this point, the earnings forecast became less central; instead a relatively stable corporate value-creation story combined with other qualitative information was perceived as being very important in valuing the company. The value-creation story, particularly where it had high historic credibility, provided an understanding context such that the fund managers and analysts could have confidence that the company would continue to create stock market value in the future as it had in the past. The story provided a means to buttress the longer-period forecasts, and provided additional information about continued stock market value. Beyond two years or so, earnings forecasts proved deeply problematic and the core value-creation story was considered central to valuation. The case companies recognised that there was a considerable leap of faith involved on the part of their core fund managers and analysts, and so a good track record and high credibility were essential to maintaining value expectations.

Disclosure structures and processes

The need for increased responsiveness and sophistication in internal and external structures was learnt by the case companies as they faced more sophisticated, global and volatile financial and information markets, as well as increasing shareholder wealth management pressures from their core fund managers.

The following case illustrates the learning process where new disclosure benchmarks, external perceptions of the quality of internal information systems and issues of external effectiveness combined to make the financial communications effort much more sophisticated. The example also shows how one company saw the 'fragmentation' of existing public 'true' voluntary disclosure in its sector (see chapter three) as a competitive opportunity to reveal major weaknesses facing its competitors.

Insurance company case

> *Our key disclosure benchmark is with our major competitor who is UUUU. This company is a major competitor for us in insurance. We therefore try to exceed their disclosure standards. We are trying to get US and UK fund managers to buy one of two of the top UK life companies and that is either going to be us or UUUU. The benchmark for effective disclosure, private or public, is sector specific. XXXX, before they were taken over by UUUU, were historically very good on disclosure; they put us and other life companies at a disadvantage in transparency. As a result of their more open disclosure, investors saw new key risks in life business and soon saw new financial ratios emerging from UUUU. Information on these was not given out from the*

other life companies. We were, therefore, embarrassed when the brokers' analysts and the fund managers asked questions based on such ratios. UUUU's price increased because it was much more transparent and it placed us at a competitive disadvantage in terms of effective disclosure, both public and private. This can be seen as the double effect of better information and better information management. The information management effect occurred because it made it clear that other life companies did not have the management information systems to find this information and then to disclose it. This raised questions about their decision effectiveness as well as what black holes might be around inside these companies. So, as you see, the quality of disclosure is a key variable and a key intangible and it can affect the stock price.

Some of the case companies had learnt that they were lagging behind in financial communication sophistication and effectiveness, meaning that they were in the process of catching up.

Property company case

A key intangible in this business now is that we are trying to improve our disclosure effectiveness. This business is now moving in the direction other businesses have travelled in for some time in improving their financial report and in their private communications to shareholders. In terms of the company reporting and other disclosures, we now seek to project to the market in a much more positive way. There is definitely a need to beat your chest now and tell the market what you are doing. Financial public relations or investor relations are very important in this era. It is now becoming very important in this sector. We are catching up with other companies who have done this sophisticated investor relations in the past. We think if we can improve the effectiveness of our disclosure, both public and private, then this intangible may improve our share price. Effectively, we are trying to show the market more about the value-creation process and the positive intangibles in this business that create value, especially in the management of existing assets and in terms of the development of new property.

In addition, the case companies developed a high readiness to prepare rapid press releases in response to changing market 'attention cycles' or 'news cycles'. The latter occurred when events stimulated a high degree of market attention on the current company story, or on a story with limited life; these could also take place in response to major changes in company financing needs, performance circumstances or new sector problems. The following case illustrates the manner in which a company learnt to respond to 'high attention' and focus on the company during the financial reporting cycle.

Transport company case

We need to tell stories of our innovation every six months for the City. We need to get and keep the City's attention … It appears that the City requires a constant feed of innovations every six months to a year. They then ask us how we have exploited the innovation a year later. When we go in to see them we need a new story or they ask us to explain how the one-year old story has worked. The fund managers log the previous meetings. They log the points we made, the promises we made and the overall story or narrative. They then check the promises in the next meeting. If they tick off the promises or points and we have delivered, this increases our credibility.

The empirical evidence in Holland (1997, 1998) and the present study highlights that companies have learnt to operate within a responsive external structure consisting of stable 'boundary' relationships between themselves and their core fund managers and analysts, set within the larger market for information. The make-up of the core contact group of fund managers and analysts that were allowed to speak only to the closed corporate group was based on a cost-benefit calculation in which top management time and eventual stock price impact were central.

The way in which the case companies tried to control the learning behaviour of fund managers and analysts within these external structures also emerged.

Technology company case

> *If you recognise that there is this learning process by the fund managers and the analysts then the company needs to take hold of it. It needs an active programme to boost the process at the right time. It needs to ensure that when events occur which match the story, then it needs to reinforce this by making sure this is well communicated to the fund managers and the analysts. We must initially tell the story very clearly and ensure that it has got a rational internal structure. We must then communicate very clearly when events occur which demonstrate this strategy is working. We must also do this, of course, when the financial results come out and they further match it. The fund managers and analysts can see this for themselves but you can further reinforce this by explaining how the story has changed through time. So, companies should not be passive on these matters, they should have very proactive investor relations and communications programmes and try, in part, to control the learning and education process fund managers face.*

Gibbins *et al.* (1990) identified passive ritualistic behavioural influences as an element of disclosure. In this respect, the case company disclosure activity was driven by financial reporting and by open and closed reporting periods. This cycle, and the stable links with core fund managers and analysts, provided the focus for regular, ritualised exchanges of information and influence where the case companies sought to control content and access. However, the increasing professionalism and control by fund managers disrupted these rituals concerning the private meeting presentation style, questions and subsequent debate. *Ad hoc* events and changing company needs and circumstances also disrupted these rituals.

The case companies learnt that board and top management qualities were at the heart of corporate financial communications.

The role of individuals involved in the disclosure process related to:

- the provision of primary information regarding the corporate value-creation process, and the way they were contributing to it;
- the provision of information about themselves in terms of their skills in managing the business;
- the manner in which they were organised to conduct financial communications;
- their reputation for disclosure honesty; and
- information about how their own pay and wealth were tied to company fortunes.

Tight control was exercised by a small top management team with sole responsibility for financial market disclosure. This team consisted of a small closed group such as the Chairman, Chief Executive, Finance Director, and professional communicators such as Investor Relations Directors. The top management group and investor relations staff received regular training and advice from financial communications consultants on how to manage their disclosure output and behaviour; scripting and rehearsing one-to-one meetings were common practices. Reputation issues were very important to the case managers. For example:

Telecommunications company case

In terms of these analysts' forecasts or estimates of cash flows then there are many intangibles here, or inputs, from the corporate side. The most important of these is the credibility of the Chief Executive, XXXX. The analysts and fund managers want to know whether he has developed a sensible strategy; they want to look him in the eyes and see if he understands the business. They want to assess or understand why he selected this strategy. They are very interested in our execution record, our execution risk. This is one of the downsides of our reputation. They are asking themselves, do we back the Chief Executive to deliver this strategy? These kind of variables are very important amongst US fund managers. Plenty of US fund managers will not invest without eyeballing the chief executive.

The case companies believed that reputation related to both personal and corporate assets, and perceived there to be a close connection between reputation (human capital assets) and financial gains (financial assets). Negative feedback from markets on their managerial skills, on the quality of their disclosure, or a rebuke from the regulator, could all negatively effect reputation and company value. Management reputation for disclosure honesty was closely tied to fund managers' and analysts' beliefs in subjective qualitative disclosures *via* the story; changes in management could therefore impact the story's status. Other external contingent factors affecting management reputation could affect perceptions of executives' management skills; this could in turn have a negative impact on disclosure quality.

The fragility of corporate top management reputation is illustrated by the following case.

Transport company case

If you think of two areas of activity, one, the world of business and two the world of politics, in each you have a reputation as an individual. A businessman has a reputation in his sphere and the politician has his reputation in his sphere. If a businessman enters the political arena deliberately or accidentally then there are many problems and conflicts that may arise. These may reveal limits and new insights into the top manager individual and these are not available in the business context. They are now in the public domain. The negative changes in the individual's political reputation may damage his business reputation. Why is this the case? I can remember the case of XXXX and his role on the government committee dealing with YYYY. His problems with this job had a very negative impact on his business reputation. Then there is the reaction of the fund managers. They think that the businessman is getting into politics. The chief executive or the chairman is not concentrated on the business job in hand. They also take the view that you pay these chief executives and chairmen very highly and expect them to be on the job for twenty-four hours. In their view he is part-time by spreading across into politics. They also fear that the rest of the company's staff will lose respect for the Chairman or Chief Executive due to their absence or lack of focus on the business. If the top management group has a close family style relationship - and it is a coherent group - then this may be lost if the main leader leaves and goes outside. The management team may be more diversified and fragmented than in the past. The new information about the Chief Executive or the Chairman may reveal that they have less control than the analysts and the fund managers thought they had in the past.

From an individual point of view, poor disclosure content and behaviour could have a longer-term effect on job prospects and on future earnings for executives. In some cases management perceived that this could lead to job and major financial losses. Opportunities for opportunism were also identified, such as if chief executives close to retirement decided to 'cash in' their reputation by using it to disclose information to boost stock prices and terminal pay arrangements. In contrast, other case company executives argued that they were very good at what they did and wished to signal it *via* good financial performance and good financial communication skills; they expected that this would boost their job prospects and ability to negotiate pay awards with the financial institutions.

There were also regulatory controls that focused on issues such as monitoring director and top manager share trades during open periods, to see whether insider information had been misused or if the manager had used prior knowledge of disclosures to benefit from share transactions. The potential reputational effects can act as a major control over opportunistic disclosure. However, the regulator does not monitor the potential abuse of corporate disclosure, whereby, a chief executive coming up for retirement may use disclosure to maximise terminal pay; the reputational consequences of doing this seem weak. However, case company executives knew that fund managers would remember such behaviour and block membership of boards in a 'post-retirement' future.

Thus, formal contracting about executive tenure and pay, as well as the incentives to perform and to disclose, were perceived as being important influences on disclosure behaviour; informal contracting on financial communications skills, reputation and credibility were considered to be equally important. Both forms of contracting interacted and affected disclosure. As a result, the case companies learnt about their reputation and credibility, as well as about the need to demonstrate their management and communication skills. The firms also learnt that they had to agree these contracts with their core fund managers through a mixture of formal negotiation and by the demonstration of a track record over time.

Once the case companies had learnt how significant top management qualities were to effective financial communications, they tried to modify these qualities through selection and adaptation. For example:

Insurance company case

> *The changes of chief executive and finance director do create new opportunities to disclose new information. The new chief executive, Mr DDDD, is an open communicative individual; he is very good at this kind of thing and this has improved our position. I am trying to get the finance director to also take this line. This is an opportunity for us to improve our disclosure effectiveness and catch up with our major bench mark competitor in this respect, XXXX. The fund managers and analysts know this and they are pressing us accordingly. In particular, I think that the analysts and fund managers are trying to find out if the new finance director has the skills and general ability to implement the chief executive's strategy. For example, does he know enough about financing the business to help us to develop our new Asian operations? This is the kind of thing that management qualities are lining up with disclosure effectiveness, and the two intangibles combine; they could well affect the information that gets into the stock price and, hence, the stock price.*

Disclosure systems

The case companies also learnt, over time, that they had to set up value-relevant information systems; they realised that they did not have perfect foresight, and thus did not know which events would occur and which precise pieces of information would be deemed value-relevant by the stock market. This uncertainty meant that the firms had to develop the means to focus on new, *ex-ante* information, which was likely to drive prices; they therefore developed information systems which were likely to do this. These information systems consisted of many elements including:

- the use of flexible, broad information categories in the value-creation process and the broad categories of intangibles;
- the seven categories of value-relevant information V1 to V7;
- a package of information (see below);
- a regular information disclosure and collection process, involving private meetings after the announcement of results; and
- a stable disclosure protocol.

All of these elements, together, constituted flexible information systems that were expected to capture as yet unknown - but specific - information items which would drive prices in the future.

As a result of the continuous interaction, the case firms created a package of information about themselves. At any one point in time, this package of information consisted of:

- the value-creation story and its narrative, both historic and current;
- the use of this story for the inferred presence of invisible intangibles and their expected value contribution relative to benchmarks;
- privately observed intangibles and their expected value contribution relative to benchmarks;
- publicly observed intangibles and their expected value contribution relative to benchmarks; and
- observed company actions, performance and consistency relative to the story and to benchmarks and, therefore, the track record over time.

The whole package of information was identified as the company-side driver of corporate share prices; the core fund managers and analysts, therefore, demanded the package in its entirety. If they only received part of the package then the companies were perceived to be at a serious information disadvantage. New information was expected to arise within the above broad information categories and to make a contribution to the share price, even if it was not clear when, or by how much.

Summary

This chapter has illustrated how multi-period corporate learning and perceptions of market outcomes of disclosure fed back into corporate disclosure that influenced current and future disclosure. This learning has revealed much about good practice in financial communications as summarised in Table 3. This feedback stimulated cumulative corporate learning and experience concerning disclosure content, behaviour, structures and processes. The case companies also learnt to build in various responsiveness dimensions into their disclosure. These included a high content responsiveness to contingent user demands, unique characteristics, changing market conditions, a flexible disclosure policy (public *vs.* private *vs.* secrecy) matched to changing circumstances and adaptable to internal and external structures. The case companies also built in dimensions of stability and persistence. Stability had already been indicated in the use of stable internal and external structures, while persistence was manifest in the perseverance with the core corporate value-creation story despite fashions and transient market demands.

This learning became the basis for a formal corporate financial communications policy. Such a policy included the corporate view about levels of opportunism and bias deemed acceptable to the market, as well as the penalties attached to excessive shareholder wealth management-deviant behaviour.

Adaptiveness and persistence were also very important to the case companies, in terms of guiding more sophisticated disclosure that was designed to: *(i)* improve fund managers' and analysts' understanding and confidence; *(ii)* reduce the effects of barriers; and *(iii)* reduce corporate exposure to unanticipated events and, hence, fragility.

Table 3 - Examples of good practice in financial communications identified in the case companies

Content

- Make the story and business model clear;
- Survey Fund managers and analysts on their understanding of company information;
- Target information towards their understanding and confidence;
- Clarify how strategy and top management are the best combination for the competitive environment;
- Emphasise information items at top of the list of factors affecting the stock price;
- Focus on positive differences from other companies in the sector and provide information about weaknesses and remedies;
- Start from the last meeting, show how strategy had been adapted and would be implemented going forward.

Behaviour

- Clarify and simplify targets and promises, and focus on delivery;
- Build in shareholder wealth management performance measures and provide timely information thereon;
- Persist in the fundamental value-creation story, despite market fashions;
- Respond to new external disclosure benchmarks;
- Recognise errors in story-telling and remedy these;
- Overcome any tendency to secrecy in the company and be honest about problems;
- Actively sell the story and build credibility - take an active hold over the fund manager and analyst educational process;
- Disclose information rapidly about changes in factors, from within the company and externally;
- Keep the city's interest through the regular feed of story developments and innovation, but take care with information concerning immature strategic options;
- Disclose concrete evidence about the story and intangibles as soon as it is known;
- Show how promises are being kept;
- Recognise fund manager and analyst limitations and preferences – tailor the value-creation story to their needs, signpost their way through key numbers, the key story elements and benchmarks.

Chapter Seven

Conclusions and Policy Implications

This report has developed a model of financial communication for large UK companies set in the context of a major world financial centre; the results provide novel insights into the nature of financial communications by the case FTSE 100 companies. The disclosure choices, the cost-benefit analysis of each choice, the use of stories and benchmarks, the observation and perception of market outcomes, corporate learning and stability, adaptiveness and persistence, have collectively emerged as a fragile, but working solution to the information gap between corporate disclosure and company valuation that exist in financial markets in the new millennium. The key elements in the model can be interpreted as tentative means for companies and information market participants to deal with the new enhanced information-asymmetry and market-valuation problems associated with intangibles during.

Field research outcomes

This report outlines an overall model of corporate financial communications comprising: disclosure choices; the story of value creation and intangibles; managerial optimism and opportunism; benchmarking; continuous corporate interaction with fund managers, analysts and stock markets; perceived market outcomes; and corporate responses. Diagram 9 breaks down these field research outcomes into four main elements of the overall corporate financial communications model.

Diagram 9 The Overall Model of Financial Communications: Market-side drivers

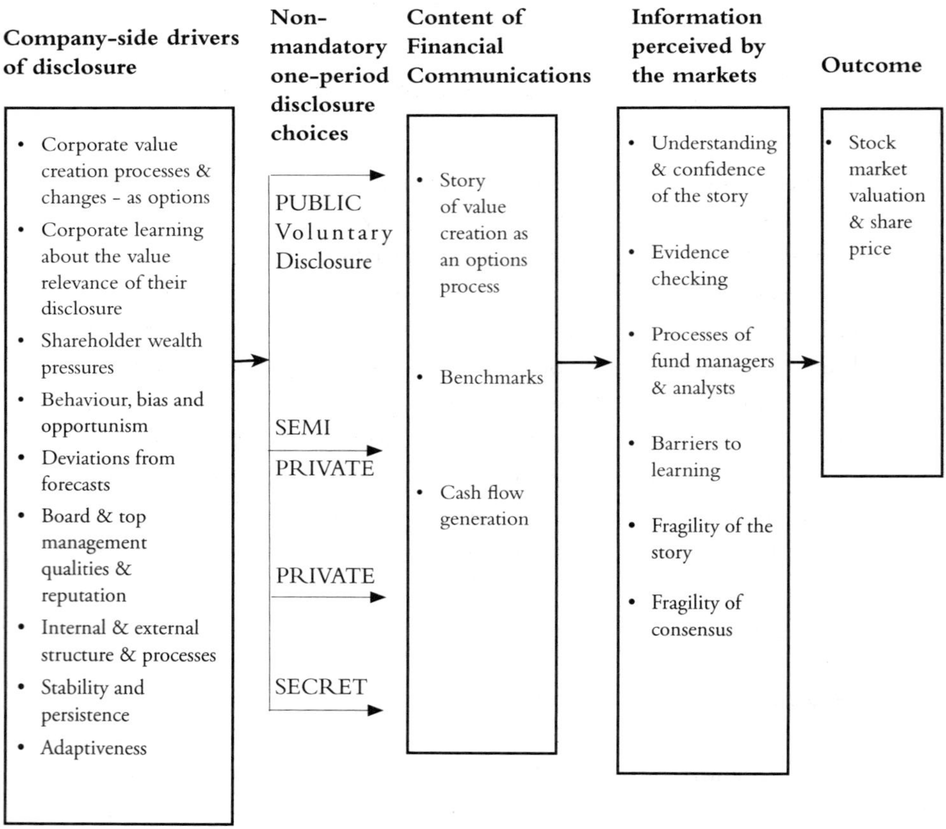

The major corporate financial communication choices in one period comprising public disclosure, private disclosure and secrecy choices were examined in chapter three, while the content of financial communications - based on the idea of a continuous options-based value-creation process - and the roles of the story and benchmarking in disclosure were discussed in chapter four. Chapter five investigated corporate perceptions of the effect of financial communications on fund managers and analysts, and how these disclosure interactions impact upon stock markets. Chapter six then analysed corporate learning about perceived market outcomes, and how this created 'a learnt context of preferences' which influenced current and future disclosure.

Each case company had a common structure to their financial communications choices, including public voluntary disclosure, private disclosure, secrecy or purposeful non-disclosure, the use of information reserves, and the limiting role of constraints. Cost-benefit calculations were at the heart of such choices; a select group of top company managers exercised these choices on disclosure mechanisms and content through a direct and responsive dialogue with individual (major shareholder) fund managers and influential analysts. The case company managers appeared to have a long-term preference for secrecy over private voluntary disclosure, and for private voluntary disclosure over public 'true' voluntary disclosure. This priority could, however, be reversed in the face of immediate short-term pressures or increased external financing needs.

Opportunism was illustrated by the priorities for public and private disclosure and secrecy choices, as well as by the way secrecy was altered by changing circumstances such as new financing or takeover bids. Opportunism was also indicated in part by the fragmentation of 'true' voluntary disclosure in the public domain and by the communication of a connected 'picture' in the private domain. The companies also displayed a bias towards optimism in their disclosure behaviour and content and for avoiding discussions of downside risks. These tendencies were 'corrected' in part by market forces.

These decisions were subject to many constraints arising from reporting standards and stock exchange rules, and were moderated by various corporate context-setting factors such as the complexity of the value-creation process. The latter also set the initial or prior conditions within which the disclosure change factors were moderated or amplified. Many company and market change situations which, *inter alia*, could increase or decrease disclosure levels were identified. However, the basic model of choice remained robust despite such changes.

Each case company built up a picture of its unique value-creation process or story using three levels or elements. These three levels were common to the cases and included: 'hierarchical' (or board and top management) value creation; 'horizontal' (or input, process, output) value creation; and 'network' (alliances *etc.*) value-creation, set in a competitive context. These three connected value-creation processes, allied to the competitive position, created important parts of the disclosure agenda for the case companies. Each company made considerable use of the value-creation story or business model as a primary communication device for disclosing information on these intangibles and for explaining how they combined in creating value. Changes in relative benchmarked intangibles were an important source of information in their own right and interacted with the value-creation story to create additional information. Both the value-creation story and benchmarked intangibles formed primary communication devices for disclosing value-relevant information. Holland (2004) provides further insight into these disclosure content issues and the role of the story and benchmarks.

A critical element of the company value-creation process was the creation of strategic flexibility; this was interpreted as a flexible and adaptive process of generating, waiting, exercising and implementing a continuous stream of strategic corporate options. The latter include the introduction of major new products, new capital budgeting investment, and many other strategic decisions. This 'strategic option' version of the corporate value-creation process and story was connected to formal valuation concepts by using an 'adjusted present value' (APV) approach. Cash flow categories were identified for each element or phase in the value-creation process and this analysis created new ways of understanding the value relevance to stock markets of information about each case company's value-creation story. Such an analysis provided a more structured means to link the information content of the corporate value-creation story more closely to the case companies' stock market communication aims.

Financial communications policy issues for companies

The main research results presented in chapters three to six of this study provide an insight into 'good practice' in corporate financial communications. 'Good practice' is defined from a shareholder wealth management perspective; it involves a selection of current practices that match shareholder wealth management aims, as well as using a shareholder wealth management perspective to identify improvements in the current practice of corporate financial communications

Chapter three suggests ways in which companies can develop good practice in financial communications to further their shareholder wealth management aims, and provides a practical frame of reference to analyse choices, cost-benefit ratios and behaviour in a static model. In particular, the case data indicates that managers should establish disclosure choices and communication channels and identify broad categories of costs and benefits associated with each choice; they should also articulate their strategic story and clarify the information that is subject to legitimate secrecy constraints. Levels of voluntary disclosure in public and private domains, and between varying circumstances (*ie.* relating to good performance, financing needs and takeover activity) should be matched to shareholder wealth management aims. The firms should also explicitly address whether their 'relationship contracting' with analysts and fund managers - and any over-optimistic biases in disclosure and opportunism - are mainly in shareholders' interests or are instead being driven largely by managerial goals.

In chapter four, the case data suggest that the broad language of strategic options, the conceptual structure of the option model and its resultant cash flows can prove useful in interpreting the corporate value-creation process and clarifying the value-relevant content of narrative disclosure into seven main categories of information (V1 to V7).

- **V1** information related to expenditure on R&D, brands, staff and processes, as well as general success in creating options;
- **V2** disclosure concerned information about the broad nature of the product market options or competitive flexibility the company was creating;
- **V3** value-relevant information involved disclosure (often detailed and price-sensitive information) announcements (at the point of exercise) about the exercise of the new option and subsequent disclosure about recent progress;
- **V4** information related to existing business such as progress in the existing business and current trading performance;
- **V5** information regarded the ability of top management to generate extra growth options and cash flows from V1 to V4;
- **V6** information concerned involuntary disclosure or external observation of how credible, trustworthy and effective top management had been as regards V1 to V5, and how effective historic execution of promises had been;
- **V7** information concerned involuntary disclosure or external observation of how credible and trustworthy the quality of corporate disclosure had been in V1 to V5.

This model provides a simple, yet clear, classification of the kinds of information that are likely to be value-relevant in the information and stock markets, and can therefore guide disclosure policy and corporate story telling about value creation. Each company should therefore analyse its value-creation process and information agenda in this way.

Chapter five describes the disclosure interaction between the case companies and the markets, and provides a practical insight for companies developing their financial communications policy. For example, information categories V1 to V5 are shown to be directly related to the information market's understanding, while information categories V6 and V7 are directly related to the information market's confidence in the corporate story. Disclosing information in this structured way provides a practical means for companies to influence fund managers and analysts and hence the stock market in a model of dynamic interaction. The chapter also makes it clear that the case companies have to expend considerable resources to: *(i)* influence the evidence checking processes of fund managers and analysts; *(ii)* overcome and minimise the effects of barriers; *(iii)* probe the information understood by these parties; and *(iv)* probe the information in the stock price. The fragility of these factors and growing shareholder wealth pressures from private meetings, and market feedback, make it clear that such actions must have clear shareholder wealth management aims.

Chapter six illustrates how this multi-period learning process, fed back into corporate disclosure and created a context which influenced current and future disclosure. Companies should seek to formally monitor and record this learning process and note how it leads to cumulative corporate understanding and experience of disclosure content, behaviour, structures and processes. A corporate financial communications policy should, therefore, be based on its learning experience as well as observation of good practice amongst competitors.

Chapters three to six develop these ideas of good practice and show how managers can jointly agree their decisions with their core fund managers and most influential analysts over time. Companies should recognise that they need to earn this 'agreement' with 'market forces' through a continuing quality dialogue with active fund managers, and by being able to interpret immediate feedback from the stock market. The central roles of private disclosure, knowledge-intensive intangibles, stories, benchmarking and many other elements in the financial communication model can be interpreted as a rational corporate response to the demands of such 'market forces' in a period when conventional financial reporting channels are facing problems of declining informativeness (Francis and Schipper, 1999; Lev and Zarowin, 1999).

Policy implications at the regulatory level

The financial communication behaviour described in this report can be seen as a regulatory success, a regulatory failure and a regulatory opportunity. It was a regulatory success in the sense that the case companies avoided the private release of 'price-sensitive information' which could immediately effect prices in material or significant ways. The case companies in the present study (and others discussed in Holland and Stoner, 1996) stripped out price-sensitive information in a structured way and announced it quickly in public; they used private interactions to focus on private disclosure concerning a deeper understanding of fragmented, more elusive information sources.

The communication behaviour also represented a regulatory failure in that it showed the deficiencies in the information content of conventional disclosure mechanisms, such as, the financial report, the OFR and public announcements made *via* the Stock Exchange. Such formal mandatory disclosure mechanisms are facing increasing regulation on their content and format, but this did not seem to match the perceived needs of fund managers and analysts and were not perceived by the case companies to provide coherent information about their new knowledge intensive economic transformation, processes and their likely impact on its future valuation. The cases suggest that this world of knowledge-intensive intangibles has developed too fast for regulators. Market forces appear to have responded to this gap and encouraged an increasing use of informal disclosures protocol based on the value-creation story, benchmarks and private channels.

The behaviour also represents a regulatory opportunity in that the above model of financial communication could form the basis of FSA-designed guidance for the three areas of disclosure: public disclosure; the disclosure of price-sensitive information; and private disclosure.

Holland (2004) argues that the central problem with the present approach to public disclosure regulation is that, at best, it can be described as *ad hoc*, incremental, and represents 'muddling through' by regulators. The author suggests that public disclosure of qualitative information should be structured on the basis of the three corporate value-creation processes, the broad categories of intangibles, the use of the value-creation story and benchmark indicators matched to their position in the story. This argument is further extended in the present study using the additional insights from chapter four concerning the status of strategic options and the seven categories of value-relevant information (V1 to V7). It is also further extended to include suggestions about the disclosure of price-sensitive information, and about further public disclosure based on private disclosures.

The research insights from corporate financial communication practice could be used in designing new disclosure guidance. Policy makers could require companies to disclose their 'business model' or value-creation story in the OFR using the option value-creation processes identified in this study. Firstly, qualitative or narrative disclosure could focus on how top management and the board play a role in creating and protecting value in the hierarchical value-creation process. This could use the three categories of value-relevant information (V5 to V7) outlined in chapter four. Secondly the qualitative or narrative disclosure could focus on how the horizontal and network value-creation processes create value. The story or narrative concerning horizontal and network value-creation could be further structured around the status of strategic options and the four categories of value-relevant information (V1 to V4) identified in chapter four. The story or narrative concerning value-creation processes could, therefore, be structured around the status of strategic options and the seven categories of value-relevant information (V1 to V7) identified in chapter four.

UK regulators have sought to improve the OFR during the 1998-2002 UK Company Law Review and in the Companies Act 1985 (Operating and Financial Review and Directors' Report etc.) Regulations 2005 which came into force in March 2005. However, the requirement for quoted companies to produce a statutory OFR was repeated on 12 January 2006.

However, this has been very much an *ad hoc* 'muddling through' approach to reform; the above proposal is more structured and offers a common, company-wide approach.

Similar comments can be made about US proposals, notably those in the FASB (29 Jan 2001) Business Reporting Research Project aimed at improving disclosure about the key intangibles driving value. However, even here the emphasis on a list of intangibles, rather than the underlying structure of value creation and the connected role of intangibles is evident. The list is *ad hoc* and likely to change over time; in contrast, in the present report the proposed use of the hierarchical value process to explore management and strategy intangibles provides a clear reporting focus for information categories V5 to V7. The use of the strategic options approach, for horizontal and network intangibles, offers a more systematic approach to reporting on the role and status of key intangibles in valuation categories V1 to V4.

Company announcements of price-sensitive information to the stock exchange could also be rationalised using insights provided by this research report. The UK Listing rules indicate many specific events that have to be announced to the market because they may trigger price-sensitive information. These include: dividend announcements; board appointments or departures; profit warnings; share dealings by directors or substantial shareholders; acquisitions and disposals above a certain size; annual and interim results; preliminary results; rights issues; and other offers of securities. Holland and Stoner (1996) identified other corporate price-sensitive information event categories from a study of UK companies. These included, *inter alia*:-

- Corporate actions (arranged press meetings) that hint at potential price-sensitive information announcements or actions/statements that can potentially reveal price-sensitive information about competitors or the state of the industry.
- Confidential corporate decisions such as pension fund changes.
- Any major company events such as re-structuring (and the associated costs), or the winning of a significant new order.
- The delay of the launch of a new product.
- Major problems in technologically intensive product development programmes.
- A move into new areas of business or plant closures.
- New developments in areas where the company is currently weak.
- The first part of a large investment programme, including its size and timing.
- New technology investments.
- Very large research and development commitments.
- Risky investments in new technology.
- Major problems or negotiations with regulatory bodies.

Many of these price-sensitive information events can be placed within two major categories identified in this study. Firstly, they could be classified as being actions and events that are associated with the hierarchical, or top management and board, value-creation process and, hence, information categories V5, V6, and V7; these would include many of the FSA (Stock Exchange) *ad hoc* list of price-sensitive information categories referred to above. Alternatively, they could be categorised as being actions and events linked to the horizontal and network value-creation process. They might also relate to the release of information about substantial changes in the corporate story, or changes in the relative ranking, or effectiveness, of benchmarked value-creation intangibles, as well as changes in the risks faced by the company and alterations to the status of strategic options. This proposal captures new kinds of price-sensitive information events and also incorporates well known types of price-sensitive information; both dimensions are set in a common and connected conceptual framework and therefore provide useful comparison points between companies. This structure overcomes the *ad hoc* character of price-sensitive information lists. The FSA Price-Sensitive Information Guidance puts the onus on companies, as well as other market participants, to regulate and control price-sensitive information flows. Holland and Stoner (1996) also noted that price-sensitive information conceptual boundaries changed with new legislation and with new case law. In addition, the concepts of information may appear clear in legal terms, but can prove very difficult for companies to operationalise. The conceptual boundaries were much more ambiguous in practice than they appeared in the law, and altered as new types of events, situations and company circumstances emerged. The above approach may, therefore, help companies deal with regulatory ambiguity by providing a clearer structure for the management and definition of their price-sensitive information. The approach may also help regulators develop more systematic ways of defining and categorising events that prove to be price-sensitive information.

Private interactions and disclosure can also be regulated in the same way. Fund managers and analysts could be asked to disclose information about their private question and answer sessions with companies, with the structure of disclosure also based on the three categories (V5, V6, V7) for the hierarchical value-creation process and the four value-relevant categories (V1 to V4) for horizontal and network value-creation processes. Regulators could ask companies to reveal which of their internal intangible quantitative, or benchmark indicators were of most interest to these fund manager and analyst users, and which external indicators were published by other information specialists, but were not generally in the public domain. Regulators might also ask companies how they assessed whether their disclosures had a positive effect on the information market and what measures or proxies were employed to gauge this.

Many of the above ideas are consistent with the prior UK development of guidance on how to disclose effectively to the stock market (price-sensitive information guidance) and how to develop good financial communications practice with fund managers. For example, the Myners Report (1995) was commissioned by the UK government on how to improve private company and financial institutional (fund manager) communications. The report advocated that private company and institutional meetings, and associated communications, should be improved in the interest of national competitiveness; it placed particular stress on improving corporate investor relations and enhancing fund managers' business awareness. A return to Myners (1995) is now desirable given the changes in the corporate value-creation process and the attendant developments in capital markets (Holland, 2004). This move could be extended to include analysts as well as fund managers, and should explore how corporate disclosure can be developed to improve perceptions and understanding by all information parties about perceived market outcomes and feedback.

Companies might be required to disclose their policies on public *versus* private choices and on secrecy. Finally, they could be asked to explain how they built in adaptiveness and persisted in this and how it contributed to a formal and explicit financial communications policy. Regulators could also demand that companies reveal how they made their disclosure information systems more adaptive to the changing demands of information markets. Companies could be encouraged to be more explicit on how their core disclosure content is adapted to various user, market and circumstances needs, and how the underlying information and disclosure systems have developed a responsiveness capability relative to ever changing market demands. In particular, companies could be encouraged to explain the principles they employ in adapting the core value-creation story to different listeners, why they change it in a specific way, and how they persist in telling the core story despite pressure to do otherwise.

Several forms of disclosure guidance, similar in nature to previous OFR, Price-Sensitive Information and Myners' (1995) proposals on fund managers and company communications could, in conjunction with further fieldwork and discussions with all the main practitioner groups in the market for information be developed from the evidence presented here. Such a development is likely to play a positive role in both improving allocative efficiency in capital markets and in enhancing intermediation effectiveness within equity savings, pensions and insurance financial institutions, as well as their internal or external fund manager or asset management functions.

Implications for research and theory

The report reveals how a grounded theory approach can develop new integrated insights into disclosure behaviour and how the resulting model is closely connected to existing disclosure theory and literature. It also reveals how new theory and literature can be relevant to understanding disclosure

The financial communications model could be extended by going outside the FTSE 100 or FTSE 250 company range, and outside the 'wholesale' market for information, *ie*. large fund managers and top brokers/analysts, to a world where disclosure is less sophisticated and where the market for information provides fewer demand-led pressures. This development could incorporate medium-sized listed companies as well as unlisted firms, and may provide stronger similarities to the Gibbins *et al.* (1990) model.

Theoretical concepts of contracting, information asymmetry, cost-benefit analysis and agency costs were viewed as being at the heart of the model of financial communications. The nature of the financial contracting and associated costs and benefits differed in their practical substance, but corresponded to broad theoretical concepts of contracting and agency costs. The discussion of this conventional disclosure theory in Appendix three reveals many potentially fruitful areas for further research such as an exploration of the manner in which continuous disclosure and financing decisions interact, and investigating how change factors, *ie.* company factors and circumstances, as well as structural change, all impact on corporate disclosure.

The literature on investor behaviour has much to offer in exploring the limitations and biases that can develop as companies disclose information to stock markets *via* analysts and fund managers. The discussion of this literature in Appendix three shows that field research on a model of financial communications is closely connected to the new research field of behavioural finance.

References

Arnold J and P Moizer (1984), 'A survey of the methods used by UK Investment analysts to appraise investments in ordinary shares', *Accounting and Business Research*, Vol.14, pp.195-207.

Barker R (1997), *Accounting information, corporate governance, and stock market efficiency: A study of information flows between* finance *directors, analysts and fund managers*, Paper presented at BAA, Birmingham, 21 March.

Barney J B (1991), 'Firm resources and sustained competitive advantage', *Journal of Management*, 17, pp.99-120.

Berle A A and G C Means (1967), *The modern corporation and private property,* revised edition, New York.

Botosan C and M Plumlee (2002), 'A re-examination of disclosure level and the expected cost of equity capital', *Journal of Accounting Research*, Vol.40, No 1, March.

Brealey R A and S C Myers (2003), *Principles of Corporate Finance*, ed. McGraw Hill.

Brennan N (1999), 'Voluntary disclosures of profit forecasts by target companies in takeover bids', *Journal of Business Finance and Accounting*, Vol.26, pp.883-918.

Bricker R and NChandar (2000), 'Where Berle and Means went wrong: a reassessment of capital market agency and financial reporting', *Accounting, Organisations and Society*, Vol.25, pp.529-554.

Bryman A (1988), *Doing research in organisations*, Routledge, London.

Buchanan D (1993), 'Recruitment mode affecting informant response', *Journal of Management Studies,* Vol.30, No.2, March, pp.297-313.

Busby J S and C G C Pitts (1997), 'Real options in practice: an exploratory survey of how finance officers deal with flexibility in capital appraisal', *Management Accounting Research*, Vol.8, No.2, pp.169-186, June.

Chugh L and J Meador (1984), 'The stock valuation process: the analysts view'. *Financial Analysts Journal*, Vol.40, pp.41-48.

DTI (2001), "The Final Report of Company Law Review", 26 July, London.

Donaldson G (1969), 'Strategy for Financial Emergencies', *Harvard Business Review*, Vol.47, (November - December), pp.67-79.

Ezzamel M, H Willmott and F Worthington (2002), *Accounting, organizational transformation and shareholder value-creation*, Working paper, University of Cardiff.

Francis J and K Schipper (1999), 'Have Financial Statements Lost their Relevance?', *Journal of Accounting Research*, Vol.37, No.2, Autumn, pp.319-52.

Gaved M (1997), *Closing the communications gap: Disclosure and Institutional Shareholders*, ICAEW, London.

Gibbins M, A Richardson and J Waterhouse (1990), 'The Management of Corporate financial disclosures: Opportunism, ritualism, policies and processes', *Journal of Accounting Research*, Vol.28, No.1, Spring, pp.121-143.

Gietzmann M and J Ireland (2004), *Cost of Capital, strategic disclosures and accounting choice*, Paper presented at Conference on 'Corporate Information Disclosure and News Management by Firms', 17-18th September 2004, Xfi, University of Exeter.

Healy P and K Palepu (2001), 'Information asymmetry, corporate disclosure, and the capital markets: A review of the empirical disclosure literature', *Journal of Accounting and Economics,* Vol.31, pp.405–440.

Hirshleifer D (2001), 'Investor Psychology and Asset Pricing', *Journal of Finance*, Vol.LVI, No.4, August, pp.1533-1597.

Holland J B (1994a), 'Bank lending relationships and the complex nature of bank-corporate relations', *Journal of Business Finance and Accounting*, Vol.21, No.3, pp.367-393, April.

Holland J B (1995), *The Corporate Governance role of Financial Institutions in their investee companies*, Chartered Association of Certified Accountants, Research Report 46, (65 pages), November.

Holland J B (1997), *Corporate Communications to Institutional Shareholders,* November, The Institute of Chartered Accountants of Scotland, Edinburgh.

Holland J B (1998), 'Private Disclosure and Financial Reporting', *Accounting and Business Research*, Vol.28, No.4, pp.255-269, Autumn.

Holland J B (2001), 'Financial Institutions, intangibles, and corporate governance', *Accounting, Auditing & Accountability Journal*, Vol.14, No.4, pp.497-529.

Holland J B (2002), 'A dynamic model of fund manager corporate governance', March, CIMA Research Report.

Holland J B (2004), *Corporate intangibles, value relevance, and disclosure content*, May, The Institute of Chartered Accountants of Scotland, Edinburgh.

Holland J B and P Doran (1998), 'Financial Institutions, private acquisition of corporate information, and fund management', *European Journal of Finance,* Vol.4, pp.129-155.

Holland J and U Johanson (2003), 'Value-relevant information on corporate intangibles - creation, use, and barriers in capital markets' - 'between a rock and a hard place', *Journal of Intellectual Capital*, Vol, 4, No.4, June.

Holland, J B and G Stoner (1996), 'Dissemination of price-sensitive information and management of voluntary corporate disclosure', *Accounting and Business Research*, Vol.26(4), pp.295-313.

Hussainey K, T Schleicher and M Walker (2004), 'The information content of the annual report narratives of loss making firms;

Preliminary evidence', Paper presented at Conference on 'Corporate Information Disclosure and News Management by Firms', 17-18th September 2004, Xfi, University of Exeter.

Investor Relations Society (2003), *2003 IR Best Practice Website Awards winners announced*, London.

Jemison D (1984), 'The importance of boundary spanning roles in strategic decision making', *Journal of Management Studies*, Vol.21, No.2, pp.131-152.

Kobrak C and P Spieser (2000), 'The use and abuse of real options for project evaluation and management', EIBA, Maastricht, December, 10-12.

Laughlin R (1995), 'Methodological themes: Empirical research in Accounting: Alternative approaches and the case for "middle range" thinking', *Accounting, Auditing, & Accountability Journal*, Vol.8, No.1, 1995, pp.63-87.

Lee T A and D P Tweedie (1981), *The Institutional Investor and Financial Information*, ICAEW, London.

Lev B (1992) Information Disclosure Strategy , *California Management Review*, Vol.34, Summer, pp.9-32.

Lev B and P Zarowin (1999), 'The Boundaries of Financial Reporting and How to Extend Them', *Journal of Accounting Research*, Autumn, pp.353-85.

Locke K D (2001), *Grounded Theory in Management Research*, SAGE series in Management Research, Thousand Oaks, CA.

London Stock Exchange (1994), 'Guidance on the dissemination of price-sensitive information', February.

McKinnon J (1988), 'Reliability and Validity in Field Research: Some Strategies and Tactics', *Accounting, Auditing & Accountability Journal*, 1988, Vol.1, No.1, pp.34-54.

Marston C L (PhD Glasgow 1993), *Company communications with analysts and fund managers*.

Marston C L (1996), *Investor relations: meeting the analysts*, The Institute of Chartered Accountants of Scotland, Edinburgh.

Marston C L (2004), *A Survey of European Investor Relations,* The Institute of Chartered Accountants of Scotland, Edinburgh.

Marston C L and J Empson (2004), *Investor relations meetings: evidence from the top 500 UK companies*, Working Paper, Heriot-Watt University.

Myers S and N Majluf (1984), 'Corporate financing and investment decisions when firms have information that investors do not have', *Journal of Financial Economics,* Vol.13, pp.187–222.

Myners P (1995), *Developing a winning partnership. How companies and institutional investors are working together*, DTI report.

Revsine L (1991), 'The selective misrepresentation hypotheses', *Accounting Horizons,* Vol.5(4), pp.16-27.

Ryan B, R Scapens and M Theobold (2002), *Research Method and Methodology in Finance and Accounting*, 2nd edition, Thomson.

Schipper K (1989), 'Commentary on earnings management', *Accounting Horizons*, Vol.3(4), pp.91-102.

Schipper K (2001), *Testing for the relevance of financial information*, Presentation at the University of Glasgow, July 12, at the 'Empirical Accounting Research Conference' 12/13th July

SEC (2000), *Regulation Fair Disclosure,* Securities and Exchange Commission, August.

Shefrin H and M Belotti (2001), editors, 'Behavioural Finance', Vols.1,2,3, Edward Elgar Publishing.

Sherman H (2002), *Presentation on Governance Metrics International,* at the 1st International Conference on Corporate Governance: at Birmingham Business School, University of Birmingham, UK, Tuesday 9 July

Shin H S (2004), 'Endogenous disclosures and the post earnings announcement drift', Paper presented at Conference on 'Corporate Information Disclosure and News Management by Firms', 17-18th September, Xfi, University of Exeter.

Sihler W M (1971), 'Framework for Financial Decisions', *Harvard Business Review,* Vol.49(2), pp.123-35.

Simon H A (1969), 'Sciences of the artificial', Cambridge, Mass.

Skinner D (1994), 'Why do firms voluntarily disclose bad news', *Journal of Accounting Research,* Vol.32, pp.179-194.

Statman M (1999), 'Behavioural Finance: Past battles and future engagements', *Financial Analysts Journal,* Vol.55, No.6, pp.18-27, Nov-Dec.

Stoner G N and J B Holland (2004), 'Using Case studies in finance'. Chapter 4 in '*Qualitative Research, 'A 'real-life' guide to accounting research*', edited by C Humphreys, W Lee, Manchester University, June.

Stopford J (1997), *Global Strategies for the Information Age,* Opening session address to EIBA Conference, Stuttgart, 'Global Business in the Information Age', 15 December.

Strauss A and J Corbin (1998), *Basics of Qualitative Research,* Sage.

Sveiby K E (1997), *The new organisational wealth: Managing and measuring knowledge based assets,* Berret-Koehler, San Franscisco.

Treynor J L (1993), 'A hard look at traditional, public disclosure, private information collection and short termism', *Financial Analysts Journal,* Vol.49, No.1, January, p.4.

APPENDIX ONE

May 2000: FTSE 250

Case	Industry	Rank range	Length of interview	Period of Interview	Position of Interviewee
1	Pharmaceutical	1-10	2 hours	9/00	FD, IR
2	Chemicals	60-70	2	10/00	IR
3	Technology	80-90	2.5	10/00	Dir Comm
4	Bank	1-10	1.5	9/00	FD
5	Oil	1-10	2	9/00	FD
6	Consumer	80-90	2	9/00	Dir Comm
7	Transport	90-100	2	8/00	FD
8	Property	80-90	2	10/00	FD
9	Insurance	50-60	2	9/00	Dir Comm
10	Insurance	10-20	1.5	8/00	IR
11	Media	230-240	1.5	10/00	Dir Comm
12	Consumer	40-50	1.5	10/00	FD
13	Technology	20-30	1.5	10/00	IR
14	Retail	20-30	2	9/00	IR
15	Telecom	20-30	2	11/00	IR
16	Utility	40-50	1.5	10/00	IR
17	Transport	70-80	2	10/00	IR
18	Consumer	20-30	1.5	11/00	IR
19	Oil	1-10	1.5	9/00	IR
20	Tobacco	40-50	1.5	9/00	IR
21	Utility	40-50	1.5	8/00	FD
22	Utility	110-120	1.5	8/00	FD, IR
23	Hire	190-200	1.5	8/00	CHAIR
24	Bank	40-50	2	8/00	CHAIR, IR
25	Insurance	30-40	2	11/00	IR

Notes: Chair = Chairman, FD = Finance Director,
IR = Various Titles for Senior Investor Relations Director

Dir Comm = Various Titles for Senior Financial Communications Director

Appendix Two

The following disclosure questions, *inter alia,* were posed to the case companies:

- How do you disclose information about intangible assets and their risks to fund managers, analysts and the stock market? *Via* financial statements, announcements, internet, private meetings, other means?
- What are the problems in disclosing such information to analysts, fund managers or through public channels?
- Will the recent changes to the Price-Sensitive Information Guidelines (UK, 1994) or the Fair Disclosure Rules (US, 2001) impede communication of information on intangibles?
- What is the role of information acquired by direct observation? *ie.* those intangibles directly observable by analysts and fund managers when employed within the company or when employed in competition in real product markets?
- How do you and how can you make choices about which qualitative information should be released *via* various channels such as financial statements, stock exchange announcements or private meetings?
- How does the combination of public and private disclosure produce more information for investors, institutional and others, and other users?
- How do you protect your knowledge about these intangible asset advantages?

Appendix Three

Discussion of the Overall Model of Financial Communications Relative to Theory and Literature

This appendix develops a discussion of the overall model using four related approaches. These discussions show the complementary relationship between this research and prior fieldwork, as well as indicating the potential for further empirical analysis. The discussions also reveal the practical limits and critical problems with existing theory in this research area. Finally, the appendix explores the potential of this work for new theory building and research and indicates how new testable hypotheses might be generated.

Field research literature

The model in this report represents a development of prior research by the author and has close links with other field-based disclosure models. The latter suggests that a common underlying field-based model may exist for disclosure across different contexts. This empirical work could be extended by going outside the FTSE 100 company range and the 'wholesale' market for information range to a world where disclosure is less sophisticated and where the market for information provides fewer demand-led pressures.

Theoretical concepts of contracting, information asymmetry, cost-benefit analysis, and agency costs

The concepts of contracting information systems, cost-benefit analysis and agency costs were viewed as being at the heart of the model of financial communications. The nature of financial contracting and its associated costs and benefits differ in their practical substance, but correspond to broad theoretical concepts of contracting and agency costs. The relevance of the theoretical concept of the separation of ownership and control was questioned in terms of understanding the flow of information from companies to fund managers. In this world of implicit contracting, companies had incentives to use public and private disclosure and secrecy to resolve the public and private information asymmetry to the cost-benefit satisfaction of both company management and core external fund managers. The same theory could be employed further to explain changing corporate factors and company circumstances, and demonstrate how these altered disclosure practices. However, the theory had difficulty in explaining the impact of major structural changes in the market on disclosure. This discussion reveals many areas for further research. For example, an insightful study could be made of: *(i)* the manner in which continuous disclosure and financing decisions interact; *(ii)* how costs and benefits match theoretical constructs; and *(iii)* the way that company factors and circumstances, plus structural change all lead to changes in corporate disclosure.

Literature on investor behaviour

The literature on investor behaviour has much to offer in terms of exploring the limitations and biases that can develop as companies disclose information to stock markets *via* analysts and fund managers. The studies show that field research on a model of financial communications is closely connected to the new research field of behavioural finance. This link indicates the potential of joint work and new theory building and research, by directly exploring the manner in which corporate disclosure impinges on, and interacts with, investor behaviour.

A discussion of the overall model using field research literature

The overall model of financial communication summarised in chapter seven represents a development of the prior work by Marston (1996), Barker (1997) and Holland (1997, 1998) concerning private corporate disclosure. Holland (1998) presents a corporate disclosure model that includes connected themes such as: the choice of disclosure channel; a private information agenda; constraints; two-way exchanges; and learning. The model of financial communication outlined extends earlier ones in terms of: the range of choices; the role of story and benchmarks; the range of intangibles involved; corporate disclosure behaviour; and more detail about feedback and changes in corporate disclosure behaviour.

As indicated in this report, the interpretations put forward in this study also bear important similarities to the seminal work by Gibbins *et al.* (1990). Gibbins *et al.* investigated disclosure processes in 20 Canadian firms and employed a similar grounded theory approach to develop a vocabulary of constructs and variables; these in turn describe disclosure processes and permit identification of relations among the constructs and variables. Diagram 9 illustrated the interaction and structure in the model of financial communication; these highlight the similarities and differences with the model identified by Gibbins *et al.*

Similar concepts, structures, interactions and relations have arisen in both pieces of work. For example, each study identifies the use of corporate communications processes to produce a wide variety of disclosure outputs in response to internal or external event *stimuli*. Both have model elements that indicate the importance of previous learning concerning disclosure. In this model, corporate learning is determined by previous interactive learning, feedback and *stimuli* from financial markets, thus revealing their joint input and output role in disclosure. Internal and external structures were major components. *Stimuli* have been divided into: *(i)* immediate *stimuli*; and *(ii)* the wide range of cumulative *stimuli* and feedback which contribute to corporate learning. Both the present study and Gibbins *et al.* (1990) place similar emphasis on opportunism, policies, structures and processes, with both studies demonstrating the potential causal links between these components. The present study confirms the significance of historic corporate learning about disclosure in the market for information and the asymmetric pay-off for disclosure behaviour in this market. Gibbins *et al.* concepts of ritualistic behaviour have also been relevant to the current study, but increasing control by fund managers has disrupted attempts by case companies to use this as a form of control over disclosure.

The research results begin to differ when specific behaviour and the structures in different contexts are examined. These UK differences included the high profile and significance of: the company value-creation process; intangibles; public, private and secrecy choices; the 'story' and benchmarking; the external structure in the market for information; and the continuous nature of disclosure. This study notes the prominence of this dynamic interaction over time, the resulting understanding, credibility, reputation and consensus, as well as cumulative learning about disclosure. The case companies perceived that the information market's understanding of their disclosures and its impact on the share price was critical in adapting company information and in developing new information. This information inter-mediation role played by the fund managers and analysts was seen as being very significant by the case companies in altering the way corporate disclosure affected company asset returns and stock market prices. The present study also highlights corporate responses to the above interaction and learning. These processes were interpreted as determining antecedents, predispositions and structures as identified by Gibbins *et al.* (1990). The differences between the studies may be attributed to the wide variation in decision contexts (City of London) for the study participants, as well as differences in the UK focus of the study (corporate value-creation and intangibles and large UK companies). In particular, the case companies faced a highly sophisticated market for information. As a result, the Gibbins *et al.* model is very useful for extending the interpretations of this case data and suggests that a common underlying model may exist for disclosure across different contexts. However, the results of this research project indicate that their framework is possibly an over-simplification; for example, not allowing for adequate change and dynamic interaction between the components, and the failure to indicate some of the reciprocity of the relationships. The comparative approach employed above can be interpreted as an application of the idea of theoretical sensitivity (Strauss and Corbin, 1998) whereby previous grounded theory generated by the author and others is used to further interpret the new case data and establish a richer model of financial communications.

A theoretical interpretation of the overall model using concepts of contracting, information asymmetry, and agency costs

Key theoretical explanations of corporate voluntary disclosure lie in the concepts of information asymmetry and principal-agency contracting (Healy and Palepu, 2001). The information asymmetry between a company and its investors arises due to the separation of ownership and control (Berle and Means, 1967). Principal-agency contracting is the means for fund managers as principals to control how their company agents use equity capital; companies voluntarily disclose information to reduce the information asymmetry and to minimise the agency costs of equity subject to information propriety and production costs.

This appendix combines these ideas in a theoretical interpretation of the overall model and of the specific results outlined in chapters three to six. This discussion reveals that these concepts of information asymmetry, contracting, and cost-benefit analysis were viewed as being at the heart of voluntary disclosure and the model of financial communications. The nature of financial contracting, and associated costs and benefits, differed in their practical substance, but corresponded closely to theory as regards the overall concepts. The information and stock market reaction could also be interpreted using these theoretical constructs. The same theory could also be used to explain changing corporate circumstances and disclosure; it had difficulty, however, in explaining the impact of major structural change on disclosure.

Contracting

In the company cases, implicit contracting, or relationships, between a company and a concentrated group of its core fund managers was perceived as the dominant form of contracting existing during periods of stability or good corporate performance. The regular meetings and interactions reflected such implicit or relationship contracting with fund managers and analysts. Implicit contracting or 'relations' can be interpreted as a form of organisational structure in that they consist of a co-operative network of boundary spanning relationships (Jemison, 1984) between companies and their suppliers of capital. Implicit contracting was the medium for many capital transactions, information flows and the forming of mutual expectations between fund managers and the case companies (Holland, 1995, 2002).

Principal-Agency forms of contracting were more evident in the case data when the case companies faced problems with their core fund managers or had poor financial performance. Such contracting co-existed with relationship contracting, with the latter forming a key information and influence for the former. In addition, the companies identified alternative formal contracting, whereby they 'rented' out their human managerial capital to fund managers; companies also acted as principals when contracting fund managers to manage company pension funds. Bricker and Chandar (2000) also note problems with the traditional theoretical explanation of separation of ownership and control (*eg.* Berle and Means, 1967) and the use of agency models to explain financial reporting. Bricker and Chandar argue for a recognition of the increased significance of institutional investors (fund managers) in understanding these issues, and portray an alternative principal-agency structure which includes fund managers. However, in contrast to the current study, the earlier analysis does not allow for the possible joint existence of a two-way principal-agency model within a relationship-contracting context.

The increased significance of relationship-contracting can be attributed to a combination of information demand-side and supply-side changes. On the demand side, there has been a post-war concentration of share ownership in the hands of UK financial institutions which has created a more concentrated form of institutional influence and control over UK companies. Gaved (1997) pointed out that in 1996 half of the domestic equities in the UK stock market were owned by just 50 financial institutions. This pattern of ownership has concentrated company and fund manager minds on each other, and increased the significance of direct relationships and other forms of private contact between them. On the supply-side, the changes have stimulated the creation of sophisticated investor relations, or financial communications. functions in UK companies. Marston and Empson (2004) reveal the degree of sophistication in 2002 and note the much increased level of activity since 1992.

The Unilever and Mercury Asset Management legal case in 2001 (*Financial Times*, October–December 2001) also revealed that long chains of accountability and contracting can exist between companies and fund managers. The chain began with pensioners and employees of Unilever, but continued with the Uniliver board and the board-selected trustees. A formal performance contract was drawn up with Mercury Asset Management as the fund manager, with a consultant monitoring fund manager performance. The chain in this case, therefore, continued into the fund manager group and the fund manager hierarchy of senior and junior fund managers, with the latter actually managing the pension fund. In this chain, the company, and its savers, were the principal and the fund manager was the agent; this reverses the contracting chains described above and demonstrates that some large companies have considerable leverage over fund managers. This in turn reveals how much more complex contracting arrangements are than the conventional theoretical models assume.

The sophisticated financial communications (or Investor Relations) practices observed in the cases, the concentration of ownership and control and the potential role of companies as principal, were at odds with conventional theoretical ideas of the separation of ownership and control (Berle and Means 1967). Relationship contracting and the sophisticated financial communications or investor relations practices observed in the cases can be interpreted as a key means of overcoming many of the separation of ownership and control problems and, hence, the related information asymmetry problems, identified in theory.

Cost and benefits; changes and disclosure choices

In the implicit contracting or 'relationship' behaviour observed in the cases the companies had incentives to use public and private disclosure, and secrecy, to resolve the public and private information asymmetry subject to the negotiated cost-benefit satisfaction of both company management and core external fund managers.

The above behaviour pattern reveals how company managers and fund managers jointly sought to manage their shared costs and benefits of corporate disclosure. The shared costs and benefits can be interpreted as a practical interpretation of the theoretical concept of 'agency costs of equity' in a relationship or implicit contracting setting. This management of the 'agency costs of equity' was conducted at both individual fund manager level and at consensus levels across the core fund managers.

The individual case company concepts of costs and benefits varied with company specific factors, such as the perceived status of strategic options, the degree of sophistication of corporate financial communications, and the corporate culture of secrecy and non-disclosure. Despite this variation, the case companies all exhibited a 'pecking order' preference, or priority, for secrecy over private voluntary disclosure and a preference for both of these over public 'true' voluntary disclosure.

However, corporate perceptions of benefits could decline, and costs increase, in response to company circumstances changing such as declining corporate financial performance, major corporate problems, or as core fund managers became more pro-active or influential. Such circumstances could, in practice, be related and act together to radically alter the cost-benefit calculations in corporate disclosure to reduce managerial incentives for disclosure and increase those for opportunism. For example, corporate perceptions of cost and benefits could be changed or reversed in the immediate short-term by dramatic events such as a major oil spill for an oil company, or by new circumstances such as an increased corporate need for external financing or by a take-over bid. In such situations, the case companies appeared likely to increase their public disclosure and to use this to discuss the issues in greater depth in private, thereby temporarily reducing their tendency to secrecy. When such a development occurred, a change in emphasis could be seen, from the implicit, or relationship, contracting of conventional disclosure circumstances, to a more one-way principal (fund manager) and agency (company) contracting environment in which the fund manager principal had more control over corporate disclosure. This change was unlikely to alter the 'pecking order', but did affect the scale of disclosure and the balance with secrecy. Therefore, the case-based, cost-benefit equation can also be used to explain the case companies' 'pecking disclosure order' during both normal disclosure and change circumstances. In both situations, the case companies had to assess the benefits less costs of secrecy *versus* private disclosure, *versus* residual public voluntary disclosure.

These 'pecking order' concepts of disclosure bear some relation to Myers and Majluf's (1984) 'pecking order' theory of financing and of capital structure. Their study views the information asymmetry between firms and capital suppliers as playing a central role in determining the nature of the financing decision; the theory is consistent with the experiences of the case companies analysed in the present study. As the case companies had to seek external financing, they sought to reduce the level of information asymmetry by increasing their public and private disclosure. Irrespective of a need for external finance, the firms continuously disclosed information to create favourable market outcomes (see chapter five); this process also created financial flexibility in the future, based on high reputation in, and access to, capital markets. This behaviour contrasts with the evidence of prior field research which indicates that companies primarily seek financial flexibility by the use of internal financial reserves and 'slack' (Donaldson, 1969; Sihler, 1971). These links suggest that fruitful areas exist for research which combines an analysis of continuous disclosure and financing decisions.

Market outcomes and new problems of information asymmetry

The case data revealed that new problems of information asymmetry arose from the development of knowledge-intensive economic processes in the case companies. Chapter four of this report extended Holland (2004) work by interpreting the company value-creation process as a flexible and adaptive process of generating, waiting, exercising and implementing a continuous stream of strategic options. This 'strategic option' version of the corporate value-creation process provided a relatively simple and structured means to analyse the value-creation processes across many companies. The valuation categories, V1 to V5, revealed that the extent of information asymmetry varied in content, character and scale, depending on various phases in the corporate value-creation process; this defined the content of the information asymmetry from the market's viewpoint.

The corporate response to this information asymmetry was shown to involve a focus on individual and consensus fund managers' and analysts' understanding and confidence and were the outcome of using evidence to test company sources. Major barriers were observed in the evidence collection and checking process. The case companies expended time and financial resources to probe and receive feedback on what information was known by core fund managers and analysts, as information was very fragile with respect to company surprises, and to changes in market sentiment impinging on company business exposures.

These case constructs can be interpreted within the information asymmetry concept as follows. Information asymmetry in the information market was the perceived information gap between corporate understanding and fund manager or analyst understanding of the same corporate value-creation process (V1 to V7) and its share price implications. The fund managers' and analysts' confidence in their understanding represented external confidence about the perceived information asymmetry. Fragility revealed the core uncertainty about fund managers' and analysts' understanding and confidence and, hence, information asymmetry; barriers exacerbated these information asymmetries. Feedback mechanisms were used to probe what information was known by core fund managers and analysts, as well as to infer what information was in the price and, hence, to assess the scale of the information asymmetry.

The sophisticated financial communication structure behaviour and the expected reduction in information asymmetry amongst fund managers and analysts was also expected to lead to benefits in the capital markets. These included a high-quality information set in the share price, a lower bid-offer spread and higher liquidity. These benefits can also be interpreted from a theoretical perspective. For example, improved understanding and reduced information asymmetry is likely to reduce: *(i)* the transaction costs of searching and monitoring faced by fund manager investors and market traders; and *(ii)* fund managers' perceived probability of adverse selection (AS) and moral hazard actions (MH) by managers with their invested capital and by traders in their buy-sell transactions. For example, transaction costs associated with the bid-offer spread can be broken down into order processing costs, inventory costs and costs of opportunism (MH, AS). The higher the information asymmetry, the higher these costs and the wider the spread. As company voluntary disclosure increases, and the extent of information asymmetry between fund managers and the company decreases, then the costs of opportunism, before and after transactions, are expected to drop, and hence the bid-offer spread narrows. This process is likely to have positive knock-on effects on liquidity and the cost of capital. The case companies expected that the stock market would build in, or discount, the above corporate disclosure behaviour and information into the stock price, and this was expected to impact on the cost of capital. Stable, high-quality disclosure, and stable and informed information markets concerning the company were expected to be discounted in the price and lead to a reduction in the cost of capital. This cost of capital 'information premium' was expected to remain stable relative to competitors with similar assets and market position but with lower quality disclosure and a less informed information market. In the same context, high company 'fragility' arose from a wide range of company exposure factors and various changing corporate and market circumstances. This fragility was interpreted as leading to a more variable equity cost of capital, compared to a company with a lower 'surprise' exposure and environment.

Prior learning and information asymmetry

Corporate preference for disclosure, was stimulated by companies:

- learning from their own actions during continuous interaction and feedback processes in the information and capital markets; and
- observing the wider change in the product and financial markets.

Chapter five of this study reveals how the fragility of understanding and confidence of the information market was more strongly linked to the disclosure of a small number of 'runs' or connected negative events. These exacerbated the information-asymmetry between companies and fund managers and analysts. The adverse consequences included: *(i)* a loss of confidence and credibility; *(ii)* large price drops; and *(iii)* increased volatility. This finding confirms the significance of asymmetric payoffs for disclosure behaviour in the market for information observed by Gibbins *et al.* (1990). A high negative payoff for disclosure behaviour was also connected to fragility, which itself related to the failure of summary proxies such as top management quality. The perception of fragility and the asymmetric payoff encouraged case managers to: *(i)* continuously monitor the understanding and confidence of the market; *(ii)* be alert to changes; and *(iii)* to ensure a rapid and informed response. The information reserves played a key role in matching these contingencies.

Constructs such as information asymmetry and contracting provide insights into the primary drivers of corporate disclosure. However, such theoretical constructs are of limited use in explaining the major structural changes in disclosure observed in the cases. Holland (2004) has revealed the company-side and demand-side *change* drivers of voluntary disclosure and the manner in which they interact. Thus, major changes in the knowledge intensive nature of corporate value-creation processes have created a new corporate information agenda and exacerbated information asymmetries with suppliers of capital. Major changes in the structure and sophistication of world markets for information, and for the exchange of securities, have changed analyst and fund manager information processing capabilities and demands (Holland, 2004). These developments have in turn combined with the company-side changes to create new information asymmetries and new disclosure problems for companies.

However, the case companies were not passive in the face of change and have learnt over time how to respond to such developments. Corporate learning about the market outcomes of corporate disclosure, as discussed in chapter five, and of the world of change, informed corporate preferences for disclosure.

The implicit contracting or 'relationships' became part of the learnt behaviour observed in the cases, existing in the regular one-to-one contacts between top company management and fund managers; it was also becoming formally embodied in regular interaction between corporate bureaucracy, in the form of the new more sophisticated investor relations functions, and fund manager bureaucracy, in the form of more sophisticated buy-side research functions. The relationship involved investment in management human capital; this context and market feedback heightened management awareness of the value of their reputation and its links to their financial rewards.

In this form of relationship, and inter-organisational contracting, the corporate aim was to use public and private disclosure and secrecy to resolve the public and private information asymmetry *via* desirable changes in understanding and confidence, subject to the negotiated cost-benefit satisfaction of both company management and of core external fund managers.

A discussion of the overall model in the context of the literature on investor behaviour and psychology

In the financial communication model the case company managers were trying to understand investor and analyst learning, the problems and barriers experienced, and the eventual knowledge in the markets.

This focus on how fund managers and analysts gained an understanding and confidence; can be related to the emerging literature on cognitive psychology of fund manager investors and analysts (Hirshleifer, 2001; Shefrin and Belotti, 2001; Statman, 1999). This literature deals with the manner in which individuals make decisions, the way they acquire, remember and process information, and how they use this to gauge the probability outcomes of their fund management and analyst decisions.

The case companies perceived that cognitive limitations existed amongst fund managers and analysts when processing company-supplied information on intangibles. The firms recognised that this led to the use of common heuristics, or 'rules of thumb', to simplify a complex world, or to deal with information overload. For example, fund managers' and analysts' commonly encountered problems with processing information about intangibles and these were 'solved' by focusing on a narrow group of key intangibles, and by benchmarking, or ranking, key items amongst these. The literature (Hirshleifer, 2001) notes that the use of 'availability' heuristics (*ie.* making judgements on the basis of what is remembered, rather than using complete data) and 'representative' heuristics, *ie.* making probability judgements based on recent outcomes rather than on many outcomes observed over time, can also create processing problems. In the case companies, the cognitive limitations of fund managers and analysts, and of their heuristics, were interpreted as adding to fund manager and analyst barriers and introducing biases (Y4) to the processing of company-supplied information.

The above problems of knowledge, and uncertainty in fund managers and analysts can be interpreted as facets of the more fundamental problem of 'bounded rationality' (Simon, 1969).

The case data revealed how fragile this understanding (Y1) and confidence (Y2) were perceived to be. The high responsiveness to changing company (Y5) and market circumstances (Y6) suggested that this reflected, in part, psychological evidence on additional market-side factors, such as individuals: *(i)* placing excessive weight on the most recent data; *(ii)* being over-confident and over-reacting (in the short-term); and *(iii)* naïvely extrapolating time series data (Shefrin and Belotti, 2001; Statman, 1999). The cases also revealed how this understanding and confidence was perceived to vary according to differing views of the same tasks and because of processing problems amongst analysts and fund managers (Y3). These findings highlight a recognition by managers of the significance of sources of biases in individual decisions, and of the variety in the cognitive limitations of individual fund managers and analysts, and how these can play a role in both creating variety in the valuation models used, and in introducing biases into information processing.

The above literature on behavioural finance has much to offer in terms of exploring the limitations and biases that can develop as companies disclose information to stock markets *via* analysts and fund managers; it also shows that field research on a model of financial communications is closely connected to the new research field of behavioural finance. Further research could seek to make these links explicit by exploring directly how corporate disclosure impinges on, and interacts with, investor behaviour.

Concepts of value relevance

Chapters four and five of this study provided rich insights into the case companies' understanding of the perceived usefulness of disclosed information. Three different concepts of value-relevant information were observed, including: *(i)* an *ex-ante* company view; *(ii)* the use of information in the market; and *(iii)* an *ex-post* stock price impact. These three connected concepts of value-relevant information all provide related insights into the kind of information that should be disclosed by companies

The company-side view of *ex-ante* value-relevant information was summarised in chapter four, *via* the seven valuation categories (V1 to V7) in the adjusted present value model of the value-creation process. This analysis revealed that the information asymmetry and value-relevant information, before it was released, was thought to vary in content, character and scale depending on various, strategic option, phases in the value-creation process (V1 to V4 information).

Chapter five revealed how, in the market for information, information usefulness was observed, discussed, perceived and deduced by the case companies. The case company observation that company managers, fund managers and analysts jointly used the story, the various benchmark measures, and the seven information categories (V1 to V7) indicated that these mechanisms and categories communicated new information. The information market focus was, *inter alia,* on *ex-ante* value relevance and its changing nature over time. On the information market side, the case companies perceived that the market-defined, company-supplied, 'value-relevant information' was partial, changing, transient, holistic and negotiated. Company information, about V1 to V7, provided in the form of fragments of information, was thought to be interpreted by fund managers and analysts in new ways in a larger 'mosaic picture'. This process was thought to generate value-relevant learning and knowledge in analyst and fund managers as well as boosting their confidence and were 'lenses' or informed contexts through which new company-supplied information and exogenous events were interpreted. Hence, the case companies employed concepts of value-relevant knowledge and of knowledge asymmetry. The growing intensity of the shareholder wealth management atmosphere in private interactions suggested that much of this transient and topical information agenda was intended by all information market parties to be value relevant in terms of improving recipient understanding, and the ability to interpret future price moving events. The information was not designed to affect the current price in a significant or material way. The companies kept to the price-sensitive information guidance, but could still release information on the 'big picture' and could seek to improve fund manager and analyst understanding. This finding is consistent with prior evidence of case companies publicly announcing price-sensitive information (Holland and Stoner 1996) and avoiding, regulator defined, price-sensitive information releases in private.

In the stock market, information was also observed, discussed, perceived and deduced by the case companies. In the capital markets, the case companies closely observed the impact of their private interactions and corporate voluntary disclosure on the publicly observable share price, volatility, liquidity and cost of capital outcomes. Other non-observable stock market outcomes such as the quality of the market information set, were inferred from an active dialogue with traders and other market participants. As a result, the case companies were continuously assessing how relevant their information disclosures were to the capital market.

This information market probing and stock market probing by the case companies can be compared with the literature on 'value relevance'. For example, Market Based Accounting Research (MBAR) and other conventional empirical research about disclosure, employs a precise, unchanging, definition of value relevance. This notion refers to information concerning observable historic events, or specific disclosures, which affects prices, or has value relevance if the historic information - based on perfect foresight - has affected historic returns or prices (Schipper, 2001). The companies' focus on stock price behaviour and its response to voluntary disclosures, is consistent with the concepts of value relevance employed in MBAR; it did not, however, employ the scientific rigour of MBAR, and was focused on continuing change within an interactive disclosure system rather than on a specific event or within a specific disclosure channel.

Nonetheless, the case company behaviour and the model of financial communications can be formally connected to MBAR and other conventional empirical research on disclosure by establishing numerical proxies for company disclosure quality, information and confidence, and then linking these, *via* hypotheses, to measures of stock price changes. Appendix five discusses how this can be done.

Appendix Four

A Discussion of the Potential use of the Overall Financial Communications Model in Explaining Market-wide Phenomena such as Mean Reversion and Asset Pricing

The main contribution of this research study has been to describe an overall model of financial communications that provides a novel 'big picture' of corporate disclosure behaviour. However, the model provides many interesting insights of importance to finance and disclosure research. This and other recent finance and disclosure studies indicate that the market for information performs a very important role in intermediating between company disclosure and stock prices, or asset returns. To explore what this role might be, the financial communications model insights can be related to the literature on stock market over-reaction/under-reaction and asset pricing. This discussion indicates the wider significance of the model to finance and disclosure research.

The financial communications model can be linked to other associated research approaches in many ways; in this section, two examples are used to illustrate this potential. First, the model's potential use in helping to develop analytic models of asset pricing is explored and second, its ability to explain important empirical results that connect disclosure to asset return behaviour (*eg.* mean reversion) is investigated.

Asset pricing

The grounded theory outlined here may be of use to academics developing analytic disclosure models. In particular, the theory could be used to develop simple and parsimonious assumptions about corporate disclosure. Analytic approaches would have to model the cumulative, multi-period learning, as perceived by companies, fund managers and analysts, arising from company disclosure; they would also have to model the nature of the information and capital market states arising from such disclosure. More abstract ideas about the nature of the multi-period equilibrium of informed states between: *(i)* company disclosers, analysts and fund manager users; and *(ii)* market prices could also be explored. These concepts would have to include the fragility of informed states and stock prices caused by random shocks.

The overall skeletal structure of such an analytic model could be as follows. In the model, the eventual company aim would be to use disclosure policy to raise information market states to a level designed to maximise the stock price of the firm. However, in a multi-period learning setting, the 'market' (*ie.* the information market, in association with the stock market) would anticipate the company's disclosure policy and fairly price the firm by discounting the company's disclosure. This scenario would give rise to a game of incomplete information (Shin, 2004), conducted over many periods. In this context, management has control over a unique reserve of information which is likely to be central to valuation, but they do not know exactly how this will affect information market states and stock prices. Over time, management learn the identity of the key corporate value drivers and the company-supplied information that normally affects information market states and subsequent stock prices; however, they can never be fully sure about what company-supplied information is in information market states or the stock price. Management are mandated to disclose periodic earnings, and face strong norms to disclose contextual information about the value-creation story and benchmarks. Information markets process company-supplied information, in a competitive setting, for information advantage and then reach conclusions about disclosure quality; this is in turn communicated to sophisticated traders. Capital markets set the price of the firm to its fair value, based on all available evidence including: company disclosures; equivalent information markets states; and the estimated remaining information asymmetry, all adjusted to reflect the observed disclosure strategy of the firm. This process would set the cost of equity capital for the firm; any remaining market uncertainty concerning company disclosure therefore relates to the way in which companies seek to resolve the residual information asymmetry. However, market disclosure expectations would set benchmarks for company disclosure and, as a result, companies would have strong market incentives to maintain high disclosure standards and to avoid surprises.

The analytic approach may therefore combine with the grounded theory approach to produce a simple model of how company-supplied information was intermediated *via* analysts and fund managers into stock prices. The game theoretic approach modelling the dynamic interactions between an informed manager of a company and sophisticated market traders can, therefore, be expanded to the dynamic interactions observed between companies, fund managers and analysts, as intermediaries, and sophisticated market traders.

The above discussion also indicates that the analytic approach should make new kinds of assumptions about disclosure. Conventional literature assumes that management know how they are priced and that they have more information about the true value of the firm than the market; they also know what the price would be if their private information was made public. However, this situation was more problematic in the cases. For example, the companies did not know exactly what information was in the information market states or in their share price; they were also unaware of exactly how company-supplied information affected information market states or prices. The case companies expended considerable resources to gain some incomplete understanding in this regard, but they knew that they were guessing about what the fund managers and analysts assumed to be in the information market states or share price.

Disclosure and asset return behaviour

If the above proposed company level model was aggregated over a large number of firms then it could form the basis of a model of wider market price behaviour. This development would involve aggregating information market 'understanding and confidence' states, and fragility effects, from the level of:

- individual core fund managers and key analysts (or the main contact group); to
- a consensus (and outliers) amongst this core contact group, all major fund managers and analysts, and at the level of the overall information market.

Chapter seven illustrated that a key to exploring some of the above questions would be the development of numerical measures for disclosure quality, aggregate (or consensus) constructs of understanding and confidence, and any fragility identified in the market for information. This advancement would allow for many new kinds of empirical tests linking corporate disclosure quality (measured using the independent qualitative disclosure measures discussed in chapter seven) to information market states (measured using the above proxies) and, in turn, stock market states such as share prices, bid-offer spreads and liquidity. Such a development might facilitate tests of how the information market intermediates company disclosures into market prices or returns.

The main questions which arise concerning aggregate disclosure and market consensus are:

- How does corporate disclosure in aggregate help create aggregate information market wide understanding and confidence states and fragility effects?
- How are market wide understanding and confidence states and fragility effects biased by systematic factors in the market for information, *eg*. short-term optimism, longer-term pessimism?
- How is aggregate corporate disclosure (*eg*. consensus forecasts) changed by systematic factors in the market for information *eg*. short-term optimism, longer-term pessimism?
- How is the subsequent adapted information translated into stock returns and asset prices?
  - does this play a role in over-reaction/under-reaction and asset pricing?

In particular, cumulative learning in the information market, by many participants, and the eventual learnt, aggregate and consensus, states may play a role in initial under-reaction, *ie.* the stock out-performs, followed by over-reaction, *ie.* the stock under-performs. Such learnt consensus states in the market for information may include higher than expected levels of initial optimism, over, say, 12 months of good news, followed by higher levels of pessimism over, say, three to five years of good news. Whatever the reason for these states, it seems likely that information market factors are implicated in the pattern of initial under-reaction followed by over-reaction.

The discussion in chapter seven about behavioural issues in finance may represent one way of exploring how, and why, systematic behavioural elements of aggregate information market intermediation processes and states play a role in biasing prices in the short-run and long-run. For example, 'good news' novelty may play a role in the short-term under-reaction, and may be based on individual psychological behaviour such as: *(i)* the placing of too much weight on the most recent data; *(ii)* overconfidence; and *(iii)* naivety in extrapolating time series. These elements may be aggregated into systematic optimism factors in overall market consensus states. 'Good news' fatigue may play a role in over-reaction in longer periods and may be based on other psychological factors which also generate systematic pessimism factors .

Connecting disclosure, information intermediation, and asset pricing

It can also be noted that analytic models connecting company disclosure, information intermediation and stock pricing are likely to be of value in developing more advanced asset pricing models. As Shin (2004) comments: 'Since earnings are perhaps the most important source of public information for a stock, the distribution of future earnings will play an important role in the determination of asset prices today. To gain the full picture, it seems essential to have an asset pricing framework that incorporates a model of disclosures as an integral part of the overall framework'. The present report also suggests that conventional (positivistic) empirical work connecting disclosure and asset return behaviour (such as over-reaction and under-reaction) and analytic model building of asset pricing, both ignore the 'bit in the middle'. This area is where the market for information processes (company) disclosure, and forms fragile understanding and confidence states.

This study indicates that new asset pricing models should focus on the joint determination of disclosure, information intermediation and asset pricing. In addition, qualitative information in the form of value-creation stories and benchmarking should also be recognised as important contextual information supporting earnings, with all information sources playing a role in the determination of asset prices.

In the company cases, information about company fundamentals was disclosed *via* information categories V1 to V7; this formed the understanding (Y1) and confidence (Y2) states in the market for information. The observed variation and adaptation of this information set during the information intermediation process (*via* Y3, Y4, Y5 processes and events) suggests that psychological factors (both individual and aggregate) and associated market conditions, are the key factors affecting information market-wide understanding and confidence states.

This analysis also suggests that asset prices are not set with reference to the company fundamentals alone, and that asset pricing models should be adapted to reflect this reality. Depending on which evidence researchers believe, and which asset pricing model is deemed to be superior, then the adaptation takes different forms.

In the case of the Capital Asset Pricing Model, the following security market line model is then no longer valid:-

$$R_i = Rf + B_i (Rm - Rf)$$

where R_i is the expected return on asset i, Rf is the risk free rate, B_i is the market beta for asset i and Rm is the return on the market.

The model could be adapted to take the following form:-

$$R_i = Rf + B_i (Rm - Rf) + C(I)$$

where:

I = fragile understanding and confidence states in the market for information

C = some behavioural factor biasing these I states and eventual returns

Thus, an equity risk premium is presumed to exist because of information market states such as those relating to fragile understanding and confidence; this premium is modified by behavioural factors.

Alternatively, a view can be taken that recent evidence supports a multi-factor asset pricing model. For example, in the Fama and

French (1996) model, company returns are a function of the following factors:-

market beta or return	+	company size small *vs* large	+	value firm high book/ market value	+	growth firm high market/ book value

It is not clear why these factors should drive asset pricing. However, the factors identified in this report, namely:

- information market factors, or understanding, confidence and fragility, *ie.* those factors which intermediate company information; plus
- information market behavioural factors which may cause short-term and long-term biases.

could be interpreted as varying according to beta, size, value status *vs.* growth status, and thereby act as the underlying drivers of asset pricing.

Similar comments apply to new empirical work connecting disclosure and asset return behaviour (for example, over-reaction and under-reaction); this requires some 'in between' modelling and hypothesis generation concerning the intermediary role of the market for information. The grounded theory outlined here provides some of the initial insights required for such work.

Appendix Five

The Generation of Testable Hypotheses and other Research Possibilities

New research could also involve the development of hypotheses for conventional empirical testing, new analytic modelling (see Appendix 4), and new connections to finance theory.

The model of financial communications outlined provides a key context for other disclosure research studies adopting quite different research methods. In terms of the hypothetico-deductive research paradigm, it may provide a wider explanatory context for market based accounting research studies, and it represents the means of generating many testable hypotheses.

The key to generating new testable hypotheses concerning this model of financial communications is to develop company level numerical measures of:

- the disclosure policy made up of a cluster of previous learning;
- the quality of disclosure (value element V7) regarding V1 to V5 and V6 information, individually or in aggregate form; and
- the quality of top management and the board as an external signal about confidence in V1 to V5 (value element V6).

These can then be followed by information market level numerical measures for:

- the constructs of understanding, confidence, and fragility.

These can in turn be connected to stock market level numerical measures of:

- abnormal returns, cost of equity capital, bid-offer spreads, liquidity and volatility.

Developing a measure of disclosure quality (value element V7) represents an important step in the generation of new testable hypotheses. Research is now appearing whereby the quality of disclosure is 'measured' using a mixture of heuristics and software such as *Nudist*. For example Hussainey *et al.* (2004) illustrate that this can be done using the voluntary narrative component of computer readable annual reports as the data for disclosure scores. The authors deleted standardised sections, such as the directors' report, the remuneration committee report, and the corporate governance report, and then identified key words in the remaining narrative associated with forward-looking information. Brokers' reports were then employed to identify profit topics relevant to earnings forecasts, and then *Nudist* was used to search for sentences in each annual report containing a specific key word. This use of *Nudist* was repeated for profit topics, for each report and the package counted the number of sentences that contained forward-looking key words and profit topics; this then comprised the particular qualitative disclosure score.

The above example represents one practical application of how specific hypotheses can be tested, and has been tailored in terms of text in the annual report. However, in principle, a common approach could be used to identify *a priori* value-relevant information (such as forward-looking information or profit topics) across a range of text sources, including: narrative in private presentations to analysts and fund managers; text in the OFR; and text in disclosures to the UK Regulatory News Service. A similar scoring approach could be applied to facilitate comparisons of disclosure quality between these public and private mediums, and to allow the calculation of combination scores for all the qualitative information released by companies.

This approach to measuring disclosure quality opens up many possibilities. For example, each measure of narrative disclosure could employ a separate figure for information quality in the various categories identified in the model. The components of narrative disclosure could be assessed by comparing disclosure quality on hierarchical value creation (V5 to V7 combined, or how top management and board played a role in creating and protecting value), with disclosure quality on horizontal and network value creation (V1 to V4 combined). Such an analysis could also employ different measures for information about various phases in the strategic option value-creation process and, thus, for the different *ex-ante* value-relevant categories V1 to V7. The quality of information could, therefore, be assessed for each phase of generating, waiting, exercising, and implementing a continuous stream of strategic corporate options. The same approach could also be used to measure the disclosure quality of the key set of intangible benchmarks, relative to a similar measure of the story disclosure quality.

Qualitative disclosure in the public and private domain could be compared, and tests conducted to determine whether private disclosure dominated public narrative (voluntary disclosures) as indicated in the model of financial communications. However, such tests would have to include some measure of how public disclosure is fragmented and how private disclosure uses a 'picture', or mosaic, approach to connect these fragments and communicate extra information.

Summary, or component, measures of qualitative disclosure could also be used to test many other hypotheses linked to capital market events or outcomes. For example:

- Do firms with higher levels of qualitative disclosure (public and private combined) have a lower cost of equity capital, lower bid-offer spreads and higher liquidity?

- Do firms increase their qualitative disclosures to counteract bad news (*eg.* earnings surprises or losses) or to respond to high information market attention during major events?
- Do firms that behave in the above fashion suffer less fragility in their stock price in the form of lower price reaction to the event, and a lower level of volatility?
- Which type of qualitative disclosures (about hierarchical, horizontal, network value-creation, or about the story, benchmarks, or option phase) play the most important role in these capital market events or outcomes?
- Does the qualitative information become more important to valuation relative to earnings forecasts as the forecasting horizon increases from 3 to 6 to 12 months to 2 years?

For example, in the Hussainey *et al.* (2004) study referred to above, the authors use the disclosure score to show that the narrative content of the annual report appears to contain greater information about future earnings for loss making firms than for profitable firms. This study could be repeated using public and private narrative disclosure to see whether the combined narrative content also appears to contain greater information about future earnings for loss making firms than for profitable firms. In a similar vein, Skinner (1994) finds that companies with large negative surprises are pre-empted by voluntary company disclosures, such that companies with bad news are more than twice as likely to pre-disclose bad news than companies with good news. The analysis outlined here could be repeated using measures of public and private qualitative disclosure quality, to determine the extent to which bad news companies pre-disclose more information. This test could also be employed to examine whether companies pre-disclose such qualitative information in a fragmented public form first, and then in a private domain in a more connected 'picture' form.

Brennan (1999) found that targets are more likely to make earnings forecasts during contested takeover bids. This form of investigation could be repeated using the Hussainey *et al.* (2004) measures of (public and private) disclosure quality to see: *(i)* if targets and predators are more likely to make such qualitative disclosure during contested takeover bids; and *(ii)* whether those that do are more successful in their defence or bidding. The findings of the present study tend to suggest that qualitative disclosures about top management quality (and the coherence of strategy) do play a central role in takeover events.

Botosan and Plumlee (2002) find that the cost of equity capital falls in the face of higher disclosure levels in annual reports, but increases in response to rises in timely disclosures. The second result is at odds with theoretical predictions, but Botosan and Plumlee (2002) argue that it is consistent with managers' views that increased timeliness increases volatility and, hence, the cost of equity. This study could be repeated to explore the extent to which companies with higher levels of qualitative disclosure (public and private combined) also have a low cost of equity capital. The analysis could also be extended to explore whether companies with higher levels of qualitative disclosure have lower levels of stock price fragility (and, hence, volatility), and if this compensates for the effects of timeliness on the cost of equity capital. Such studies could be usefully extended to explore the relationship between levels of qualitative disclosure and bid-offer spread or liquidity.

Gietzmann and Ireland (2004) argue that Botosan and Plumlee's (2002) evidence of the cost of equity capital increasing in response to timely disclosures may be caused by correlated omitted variables contaminating the results, or it might instead reflect problems relating to disclosure measures. The authors argue that accounting policy choice is likely to be a key omitted variable, with aggressive accounting policy choices leading to a higher cost of equity capital. In the study, such choices are controlled for, and a new measure of timely disclosure is constructed that attempts to measure the quality of company perceived price-sensitive information disclosures to the Regulatory News Service of the London Stock Exchange. The study finds that the cost of capital decreases with timely disclosure, but the relationship is only significant for firms using aggressive accounting techniques, suggesting in turn that such timely disclosures are needed to compensate for their perceived aggressive accounting problems. Conservative accounting firms benefit from a lower cost of capital that is unaffected by timeliness.

Chapter four of the present study also indicates that the cost of equity capital may be determined by confidence factors associated with the hierarchical value-creation process. The latter involved variables such as the quality of top management and the board. In the context of this research report, the Gietzmann and Ireland (2004) use of measures of aggressive or conservative accounting policies can be interpreted as the use of publicly observable proxies for learnt priors regarding disclosure opportunism and bias. These were built into case company disclosure behaviour and policy and were a component of top management qualities as perceived by fund managers and analysts, or value component V6.

The evidence provided in this report, and the earlier studies discussed above, suggests that at least three variables - top management quality, disclosure quality, both public and private, and timely disclosures - interact in novel ways to affect the cost of equity capital, assuming that underlying asset risk does not change. Thus, the Gietzmann and Ireland (2004) study could be repeated to explore whether perceived quality levels of qualitative disclosure (public and private combined - as in the V7 value element) are associated with public rankings of top management quality (value element V6) and whether these interact to affect the timeliness of disclosure in some way. The study could then usefully proceed to explore whether these interactions have differing impacts on the cost of equity capital.

The financial communication model might also prove useful in terms of identifying new 'intangibles' events which have information content; these could include observed changes in intangibles benchmarks such as management quality, or R&D effectiveness. It may be difficult to test for the 'information effect' of a change in the value-creation story or its narrative, but it may be possible to observe story changes, and for these to be followed by observable changes in absolute and relative benchmarks, which are themselves followed by a price reaction. Clearly lags or delays would have to be built into the tests to capture the story change and then the benchmark changes. One approach could be to adapt the Hussainey *et al.* (2004) approach to measure the disclosure quality of the key set of benchmarks, and then to compare this with a similar measure of the story disclosure quality. This method would allow for measurement of changes in both benchmarks and story narrative, and thus create opportunities to test for relative information content. Such tests are required to establish if the story change has information content or if, instead, the story is an empty ritual, employing an informationally neutral set of symbols. The model of financial communications may also be of help to existing event study research. Such event studies may be placed within the context of continuous corporate disclosure and, therefore, help identify other events and processes obscuring the information content of the chosen event.

A second way of generating new testable hypotheses would be to develop numerical measures for the constructs of understanding, confidence and fragility identified in the market for information. Surveys of analysts and fund managers could be based on the qualitative disclosure measures discussed above - their views and relative rankings of companies could be used as proxies for consensus understanding levels in information markets. Another numerical proxy for consensus understanding could be the number of company intangibles being ranked (publicly or semi-publicly) by survey companies, or by groups such as the Investor Relations Society. The rankings across many intangibles, compared to competitors, could be used as proxies for consensus market confidence in the company value-creation story. Market consensus confidence in top management could be proxied for by information market relative ratings of top management and their strategy.

The cases indicated that higher perceived quality of consensus understanding states and the consensus confidence states (concerning qualitative factors such as the current corporate value-creation story) were expected to positively influence the consensus, and variation around, expected earnings and other forecast accounting and finance numbers. High levels of perceived market understanding and confidence in the company value-creation story were therefore expected to increase the expected values and reduce the variance around consensus forecast earnings, all others things being equal. The existence of these relationships suggest in turn that new numerical proxies can be established here. For example, the expectation would be that historical average variance of earnings consensus numbers would be low for firms that score high on the above historic consensus for understanding and confidence. Firms that perform well on the basis of these measures should be expected, other things being equal, to have more accurate consensus earnings forecasts over a period of time. The variance in this variance should be close to zero, centred around a low, but positive, average value. Over time, therefore, the variance of earnings forecasts of such firms should also be low - and exhibit less variation - than firms with low scores for these consensus understanding and confidence measures. If such a relationship can be established, then 'average variance' and 'variance of variance' of earnings forecasts could be useful numerical proxies for consensus understanding and confidence states in information markets.

This approach would facilitate many new kinds of empirical tests linking corporate disclosure quality (measured using the independent qualitative disclosure measures discussed above) to information market states (measured using the above proxies), and then stock market states (such as share price, bid-offer spread and liquidity). This framework might also permit tests of how the information market intermediates company disclosures into market prices or returns.

If such proxies exist then measures of qualitative disclosure could be combined with information market understanding and confidence measures, and be used to test many other hypotheses linked to company disclosure, information market states and capital market events or outcomes. For example:

- Do firms with higher levels of qualitative disclosure (public and private combined) have higher levels of information market understanding and confidence, and a lower cost of equity capital, lower bid-offer spread, and higher liquidity in the stock market?
- Does high company 'fragility' arise from a wide range of company exposure factors and various changing corporate and market circumstances? Does it lead to a more variable equity cost of capital, compared to a company with a lower 'surprise' exposure and environment?
- Do firms with higher quality information market states face less bad news? Do such firms respond to bad news in a different way to (higher disclosure) firms with poorer information market states? Do firms that differ in these respects have different levels of 'fragility', where fragility can be measured by a proxy such as variability in the cost of equity capital (where a positive relationship would be expected). Do firms that differ in these ways have a lower/higher price reaction and lower/higher volatility in response to a 'bad news' event or to high information market attention during major events?
- Which type of qualitative disclosures (about hierarchical, horizontal and network value-creation, or about the story, benchmarks or option phase) play the most important role in determining information market understanding and confidence states, and in related capital market events or outcomes?

- How does boosting qualitative corporate disclosure when raising finance in capital markets (or during contested takeover bids), alter: *(i)* understanding and confidence states; and *(ii)* (if at all) the financing or takeover outcomes?
- Does the information market practice of mediating aggregate company disclosure influence - or cause - 'over reaction', 'under reaction' and mean reversion in stock markets? The same approach could extend tests of the degree to which aggregate disclosure is a factor in asset pricing models (see Appendix 3 for further discussion of this issue).

A third way of generating new testable hypotheses would be to develop a numerical measure for a communications policy variable consisting of a cluster of learned priors for disclosure choices (as well as content, opportunism and bias) and the stability, adaptiveness and persistence dimensions in such priors. Such a measure could be based on a defined set of financial communications policy variables that are assigned a value for each company and then combined into a summary disclosure policy score. If such a disclosure policy measure could be defined and measured, it could then be combined with information market understanding and confidence measures and be used to test many other hypotheses linked to disclosure policy, information market states and capital market events or outcomes.

Finally, the model captures information flows of relevance to many corporate finance decisions. Chapter four of this report illustrated the ways in which the companies used the story narrative to disclose information about cash use and generation categories at various phases in the continuous option value-creation process; these in turn netted out to form the cash for distribution to external suppliers of capital. Such a model may potentially be combined with an investment-financing cash flow model of the firm (*eg.* Brealey and Myers, 2003) to add a novel and dynamic information dimension to the conventional corporate finance view. For example, the main areas of use of cash flows (as well as sources of new cash flow generation) can be matched to various stages in the value-creation story. In addition, the story elements can be matched to internal and external cash flows with capital markets; changes in such flows would be central to valuation.